* 1

PRAYERS

Maria Valtorta (1897-1961), an Italian mystical writer, is famous for her major work on the life of Jesus, published in an English version entitled *The Poem of the Man-God*.

The selections included in this small volume, entitled *Prayers,* have been taken from her "minor" works, two of which, the *Autobiografhy* and *The Book of Azariah*, are now available in English.

Maria Valtorta

PRAYERS

CENTRO EDITORIALE VALTORTIANO

Original title: *Preghiere*

Texts selected by Emilio and Claudia Pisani.

Translated from the Italian
by Giovanni Liani and Doris J.M. Ballard.

ISBN 88-7987-018-1

Filmsetting by Centro Editoriale Valtortiano srl.

Cover design by Piero Luigi Albery
Photography by Nicola Giuseppe Smerilli

Printing by Grafiche Dipro, 31056 Roncade, Italy

Printed in Italy, 1995

INDEX OF TITLES

Entreaty

Offering

Meditation

Entreaty

"O holy Word"

December 7, 1943.

Mary says:

" ...He could well have come to earth and been Evangelizer and Redeemer without lowering his incarnate Divinity to the natural necessities of a child. In the same way as He rose to heaven after his Mission, he could have come down to begin it with a body that was adult and perfect, necessary to your carnal sluggishness. My Lord and Son can do everything, and I was only an instrument to help you to better understand and become more convinced about the real Incarnation of God, most pure Spirit, under the identity of Jesus Christ, the Son of Mary of Nazareth. The achievement of having obeyed the Word of God and of having sharpened the sensitivity of my soul with a total purity since my infancy, that was greatness; and the act of having listened to the Word that was my Son so that He would be my bread and I would form one being only with Him, that was beatitude."

O holy Word!

Gift granted to those beloved by God, fiery mantle that covers with splendor, life that becomes Life for those to whom You give Yourself, be always more loved by them, as I have loved You with ardor and humility.

Be active in my sons, O most holy Word, because I, whose adored Son has been killed, have accepted them as my own at the foot of the cross to comfort my Mother's broken heart, and lead them to heaven by a road of resplendent truths and ardent works.

Bring them to my Heart, where You slept as a Babe and rested once You had died, where drops of your precious Blood and the traces of my tears can still be found. With this touch, may what is still human in them disappear, and may they, resplendent in your light, enter with You the City where everything is eternal perfection, and where You reign and will reign, O my most holy Son!"

December 11, 1943.

The same prayer recited by the faithful:

O holy Word!

Gift granted to those beloved by God, fiery mantle that covers with splendor, life that becomes Life for those to whom You give Yourself, may You be loved more and more with ardor and humility.

Be active in these children. They are yours and Mary's; she has accepted them as her own at the foot of the cross to comfort her Heart as a Mother whose adored Son has been killed, and to glorify your divine Heart, O most holy Word of my Lord God!

Bring them to your Heart and to the Immaculate Heart of Mary, your Mother, where You slept as a Babe and rested once You had died, where drops of your precious Blood and the traces of her maternal tears can still be found. With this touch, may what is still human in them disappear, and may they, resplendent in your light, enter with You the City where everything is eternal perfection and where You reign and will reign, O holy Son of God, Word incarnate of the Father.

"Mary, unveil the secrets of your Heart to me"

February 14, 1944.

... One of my prayers, which came spontaneously from my heart after having recited the one that is written under the image of the Immaculate Heart:

Very tender Mother, unveil for us the secrets of your Immaculate Heart. Cause one of your most gentle and pure rays to penetrate our hearts, transform them and prepare them for the divine visits of the Holy Spirit.

I had added:

Yes, Mother of Jesus and my Mother, unveil the secrets of your Heart for me, and prepare mine with your light.

My poems for Jesus and Mary

May 13, 1943, (in the morning).

On Good Friday [of 1942], I saw the crucified Jesus for the first time... A vision that lasted over many months, not in a continuous way, but frequently... In the month of June, I wrote the following poem under this impression. For years I hadn't been up to writing poetry because I was suffering so much that poetic inspiration had dried up like a flower that had died. I am copying it here for you, not because I consider it a masterpiece, but because it well expresses my impressions after that vision, and explains them better than my own phrases done in prose. Immediately afterwards, I also wrote the one to the Blessed Virgin... I will copy them both for you.

Sinister is the mountain, barren the peak.
Heaven, Lord, darkens over your suffering,
while, for us, on the heights
You spend your blood drop by drop.
    Your open arms form a cross,
    your head is bowed beneath the crown
    your look is veiled, your voice is silent,
    only your heart is alive, driven by love.
You look at the hatred and the wars of men
who, on their fatal course, sow with pride
famine and debris upon all of the earth.
Mankind, Lord, always prefers Harm,
    rather than Goodness, Peace, Love, Faith:
    this Goodness which is your Son, this Peace
                [which is a holy flower
    from the gardens of heaven; this Love that
                [silences
    all egotism, and this Faith, only life of the people.
Host, who buys back all of our hurts, yes,

You climb Calvary yet one more time
and You give yourself up for us, for us You suffer
on this wood that rises up into the sky.
　　Why, Lord, why are You
　　once more upon the sorrowful cross?
　　Man, enraged by his passions and his lusts
　　works against himself and will not admit defeat
before becoming mud again
from whence You brought him out for a higher destiny.
He throws himself against You, O Christ,
driven by a blind and mortal fury.
　　And yet, for man who insults You,
　　again You repeat your gesture of expiation
　　so that You can become a lightning rod for us
　　against the terrible bolts of your Father.
Alone, naked and wounded, raising your voice to
[heaven
You say: "Everything is finished! Forgive them again
for this hour. Give them Paradise!
I have redeemed them once again!"

June 16, 1942

To the Virgin Mary

Ave Maria! You that are so holy,
gentle Mary, you that are filled
with grace in such a large measure,
　　protect this devout youth.
You, blessed among all creatures,
through the love of the Lord who is with you,
protect her from every pitfall
　　and against somber days of distress.
Through the love of this merciful Child
that you carried in your virginal womb,
turn your look of love towards us,
　　O Queen of hearts that suffer.

Holy Mary! Pray for us mortals.
O Mother, without you our life is like
a lost swallow, with wings tired
from the extreme effort of a voyage that was too
[long,
or of a small boat which the fury of the unleashed
[waves
shakes in every direction, in every way.
You who are the star of the sea, calm my storm
above the raging waves.
In our life, and even more in the hour
when for us, the lights will be extinguished
in the obscurity of death, you, Virgin and Mother,
open the eternal gates for us and conduct us to
[God.

June 17, 1942

I am happy to have composed my two last poetical works for Jesus and Mary. Even if the rhymes are awkward, it doesn't matter. Jesus gives me a good grade in spite of it all, because He looks at the love far more than at the meter and rhyme.

"I adore, O Jesus, your five Wounds"

[Transcription of February 9, 1946.]

My two little rosaries to the five Holy Wounds.

Adoramus Te Christe et benedicimus tibi, quia per Sancta Crucem tuam redemisti mundum.

I adore, O my Jesus, the most Holy Wound of your right hand and I beg you, for the sake of its pain, to grant me the spirit of charity. *Our Father, Hail Mary, Glory Be.*

I adore, O my Jesus, the most Holy Wound of your left hand and I beg you, for the sake of its pain, to grant me the spirit of contrition. *Our Father, Hail Mary, Glory Be.*

I adore, O my Jesus, the most Holy Wound of your right foot and I beg you, for the sake of its pain, to grant me the spirit of apostolate. *Our Father, Hail Mary, Glory Be.*

I adore, O my Jesus, the most Holy Wound of your left foot and I beg you, for the sake of its pain, to grant me the spirit of sacrifice. *Our Father, Hail Mary, Glory Be.*

I adore, O my Jesus, the most Holy Wound of your chest and I beg you, through love for it, to accept my offering as victim of divine Justice and of your merciful Love. *Our Father, Hail Mary, Glory Be.*

O my Jesus, for the sake of the suffering that pierced your holy and immaculate body, and in the name of your love I beg You to grant me what I ask of You.

Strengthen me with the holiness of the Blood that flowed from your Wounds, purify me with the water that flowed from your open heart. Set my soul afire with the splendor of your divine wounds. Cause the rays of love that shine from them to pierce my heart with ardent arrows, and imprint there the image of your pierced Body so that I may become one who is crucified by love.

Through the love of your most holy Wounds, give me a thirst for You that is more and more ardent. Allow me to be transformed in You. Grant me an ever more scorching charity, capable of washing away my sins so as to make me ready for heaven.

One other little rosary to obtain resignation.

Adoramus Te Christe et benedicimus tibi, quia per Sancta Crucem tuam redemisti mundum.

I adore, O my Jesus, the most Holy Wound of your right hand and I beg you, through love for it, to grant me the gift of resignation in physical sufferings. *Our Father, Hail Mary, Glory Be.*

I adore, O my Jesus, the most Holy Wound of your left hand and I beg you, through love for it, to grant me the gift of resignation in moral sufferings. *Our Father, Hail Mary, Glory Be.*

I adore, O my Jesus, the most Holy Wound of your right foot and I beg you, through love for it, to grant me the gift of resignation in spiritual sufferings. *Our Father, Hail Mary, Glory Be.*

I adore, O my Jesus, the most Holy Wound of your left foot and I beg you, through love for it, to grant me the gift of resignation in suffering, sorrow, discouragement due to illnesses, insults, treachery, reversals and the ingratitude of creatures. *Our Father, Hail Mary, Glory Be.*

I adore, O my Jesus, the most Holy Wound of your chest and I ask you, through love for it, to grant me resignation in death. Even more, I ask You for calmness, peace, joy at the moment of death. Grant me, I beg you, to be able to die in an outburst of love for You.

Our Father, Hail Mary, Glory Be.

"O most divine Blood"

June 28, 1943.

Jesus says again:

" ... During the month that is about to finish, I have spoken a lot to you about my Heart and Body in the Sacrament. Now, for the month consecrated to my Blood, I will make you pray to my Blood. You will thus pray in this way:

O most divine Blood that was shed for us from the veins of the God who became man, descend like a dew of redemption upon the contaminated earth, and on the souls that resemble lepers because of sin.

Behold that I receive You, O Blood of my Jesus, and that I pour you out upon the Church, on the world, on sinners, on Purgatory.

Help, comfort, purify, inflame, penetrate and fecundate, O most divine Seed of Life. May indifference and error not prevent your stream from flowing. On the contrary, for the tiny number of those who love You, for the infinite number of those who die without You, quicken and spill upon us all this divine rain so that, full of confidence, we may come towards You in this life, be forgiven by You at our deaths, and be admitted with You into the glory of your Kingdom.

Amen."

"I have desired You, Eucharistic-Jesus"

October 27, 1943.

Jesus says:

" ...The churches where I am left alone are numberless. In spirit, come into them. Learn how to compensate for the lack of other people's love. Let Me teach you to say:

I have ardently desired.

I have ardently desired to come towards You, Jesus, condemned to live all alone on such a large number of altars, to tell You that I love You with everything that I am.

I have ardently desired to come see You, O my Eucharistic Sun.

I have ardently desired to eat the Bread that You are for me. For this great desire, have pity on your servant, Lord.

Let me come to the celestial altar to adore You eternally, O Lamb of God.

O divine Sun, grant that, in a rapture of my soul, I see You in the midst of your glory, because now You appear to me as hidden by the veil of my human condition, which causes me to be weak.

Let me love You as I would like to love You for a joyful eternity.

Open for me the gates of Life, O Jesus, my life.

Come, Lord Jesus, come.

In the communion of Light, may what is flesh perish, and may the spirit conquer You, my Triune God, the only love of my soul."

"I adore You, O Jesus, in the scattered hosts"

June 4, 1943.

Jesus says:

" ...You know, and you think about it with sorrow, that many hosts are scattered in the dirt and the ruins of devastated churches. It's as if I Myself was crushed, because I am present in the Sacrament. Well, with your thought, you can use your love as a precious carpet or like a most pure linen cloth to gather Me up in my Holy Eucharist. I am stricken, wounded, profaned, driven from my tabernacles.... Accept to say this prayer many times a day:

Jesus, struck in our churches by satanic power, I adore You in all of the scattered and destroyed hosts in the debris and dirt of the ruins.

Take me as your ciborium, as your throne, as your altar.

I know that I'm not worthy of it, but You like to live among those who love You, and I love You for myself and for those who don't love You.

May sorrow clothe me with his blood-red garment so that I may become a ciborium worthy of You, who would desire to be like us in this time of war.

May my love be a lamp that burns before You, O Most Holy One, and may my holocaust be an incense.

Amen."

"May your kingdom come, Lord"

October 22, 1944.

Prayer dictated by Jesus for the Octave of the Feast of Christ the King.

Jesus, King of Love, have mercy on us.

Since we want to love You, help us to love You.

Since we recognize that You are the true King, help us to know You better all the time.

Since we believe that You can do everything, confirm our faith with your mercy.

You, King of the entire world, have mercy on this poor planet and on us who are settled here.

You, King of peace, give peace to the world and to us.

You, King of heaven, grant that we may become citizens of your kingdom.

You know that we cry: console us.

You know that we suffer: ease us.

You know our every need: help us.

We are aware of being the authors of our own suffering, but we hope in You.

We know that the suffering we live is very little compared to what we would merit, but we have confidence in You.

We know what we did to You, but we also know that You have done for us.

We know that You are the Savior: save us, Jesus! O King crowned with thorns, by this martyrdom of love, be the Love that brings help for us.

With your pierced hands, open for us the coffer of the treasure of Grace, and of all the other graces.

Come towards us with your wounded feet. With the

blood that runs from your wounds in precious drops which prove your Royalty as the Redeemer, sanctify the earth, and with it, all of its inhabitants.

Open our hearts to love with the flames of your heart open for us.

If we love You, we will be saved, now, at the hour of our death, and at the Last Judgement.

May your Kingdom come, Lord, on the earth, in heaven and in our hearts.

"Save us, Mary, from the fury of our enemies"

June 5, 1943.

Prayer to Our Lady of Sorrows.

Mary, you took us as your sons at the foot of the Cross. Mary, as our Mother and the Mother of Jesus, our brother and our God, listen to the voice of your children.

Behold, we drag ourselves to the foot of the Cross where your Son is agonizing, and where you live your agony, O Mother, with your heart broken by the spectacle of the death of your Creature.

Look at us, Mary. We are all touched by the Blood of your Son. He died for us, to give us Life and Peace in this present world and in the one that awaits us. Now we are turned towards You who have been the first stone of our redemption. We turn towards You so that we may have life, salvation and the peace that we lost because of the spirit of rebellion that we have allowed to enter our lives, and because of the denial with which we have opposed your Son's doctrine.

Yes, we know that we deserve the scourge that strikes us. We humbly recognize it in the hope that by this gesture, we will establish a resemblance to You, who were the Most Humble and the Most Pure. But besides being pure, O Mother, You are also merciful. So treat us with mercy, O Mary, who gave birth to Mercy personified!

Save us, save us, O Mary, from the fury of our enemies!

Save our churches and our houses, the churches and the houses of this village that recognizes You as Queen and Holy Patroness.

Save our men, these men that You have so often saved from the sea's gales, O Star of the Sea.

Save us who are prostrated at your feet; save those whom sickness prevents from coming here, but who are here spiritually through their desire and their suffering.

Save also those who are conspicuous in their absence, those that have been prevented from coming by ill will, the lost children, the wicked, the most wretched, those who have rejected the Light, the Way and the Life, by rejecting your Son, who is absolute Truth.

And to penetrate your merciful Heart with our prayer, behold that we are giving up, O Mary, all resentments and all instincts of vengeance. We don't want to be cruel, even if we are the victims of the cruelty that others demonstrate towards us.

In this hour we remember that we were all created by the Father who is in heaven, that we are brothers of the Son, and that we are all loved by the Spirit.

In this hour we remember the prayer of your Son Jesus, who was immolated for us: "Father, forgive them," and we repeat it for everyone, on everyone, to be able to be pardoned by the Eternal Father in our turn, and thus know salvation thanks to You.

Ave, O Maria! From your pierced Heart let fall on us the grace of salvation for this little village, for our country, and for the entire world that is dying amid the ruins that were brought about by its rejection of heaven.

Holy Mary, pray for us. And if by God's will we are destined to leave this mortal life soon, be beside us at the hour of death to bring us with You, O Mary, there where we will be able to see You and thank You in the eternal light of God.

Amen.

"Give us peace, O Mary"

In this dark hour when so many people are crying amid the ruins of their country, where so many houses, so many affections and so many dreams fall into pieces under the storm of a chastisement that is deserved, but terrible, with consciences clouded over by our errors and by our grief, we supplicate heaven, and You, O Queen of heaven.

May the light of divine Grace descend upon us and bring us the wisdom to understand what really is necessary, and make us capable of asking for it. May it descend to enlighten our hearts which have lost the science of Life and no longer know how to do much of anything, except commit sins. May it descend to teach us prayer and love.

We have a great need for love and prayer. We no longer know how to love and how to pray, how to allow ourselves to be guided by a true faith in God and by a sincere love for Him and for the brothers He has given us. We no longer know how to love and pray, and that is where all of our troubles began.

In place of a heart, we have a knot of hatred and of sin. Our soul, like a bird caught in the net of a bird hunter, is no longer able to rise towards heaven. It agonizes in contact with the mud of the earth.

O Mary, You who were able to obtain the grace of having the water in the jars changed into wine, help us to obtain the most important miracle: the conversion of our hate-filled hearts into love. Rid us of this tendency, which makes us resemble Cain, O Mother of God, who are also our Mother.

By this divine maternity, which forms the double crown, immaculate and virginal maternity, become Mother a second time of this poor humanity which is dying, strangled by the one that You are crushing with your heel, who is taking vengeance on us, weak and blind, for the defeat he suffered through You, O Most Powerful.

Allow the Holy Spirit to impregnate You a second time with love so that You may give birth to us anew to life and to grace.

If we can be born again in You, we will take from your Heart the purity that we have lost, and the charity that makes us sons of God. We will thus know how to lift our hearts, and become able to do so in a prayer that will not be the simple sound of empty words, but a true act of faith, and the sincere expression of our desire to become holy.

Teach us to pray and to love, O Mary.

Guide our souls and the movement of our lips, O holy Virgin, so that we may ask for the peace of which You are the Queen and the Treasurer, being the Mother of the Christ, who is Peace personified.

Teach us to ask for and to deserve the peace that brings children back to their parents, husbands to their wives, fathers to their children, peace that makes us become good and hard working, the peace that permits nations, now divided, to become reunited under the sign of your Son, who told us to love one another as brothers, and who has Himself loved us like a brother by giving his life for us.

Peace, O holy Virgin! Through your glorious Assumption, give us peace, O Mary!

So that those who already accept and love You, not as You deserve, but as they can, come to accept and love You twofold. So that those who don't know You as You really are come to believe in You. And those who don't know or don't want to know who You are come to accept You.

O Morning Star, be again the visible light which crosses our heaven, this heaven which is polluted by our explosions and profaned by our curses.

With your smile, banish the nightmare that has spread itself over the world and that removes from the sons of

Adam the certitude of God.

Protect us, O Queen, against dangers of all kinds, and protect the mission of your Son, who came to bring peace to the world at the cost of his suffering. One day You said: "Let it be done according to the word of God," and these words determined the beginning of salvation for the human race.

Oh! Tear for us the word of peace from the Eternal One, in remembrance of the instant that saw You joined to the Most Holy Trinity.

Cause the divine lips of your Son to pronounce this blessed "Fiat," so that the din from all these instruments of death will cease, and the hymn that celebrates the goodness of God and your power, O glorious Virgin, may rise towards the Most High's throne and your own.

...This is what presented itself today. I wrote it down....

August 13, 1943.

"Jesus, forgive our sins and be the sole occupant within us"

May 26, 1949. Ascension.

Jesus, loving in an even more extraordinary fashion, wants to comfort me with his love, to comfort me for many things. His infinite charity, so sensitive, plunges me into a contemplation on all of my problems, past and present, and into a sorrowful contrition so great that I've never felt the like before. Even if Jesus were not there to confirm it, I feel that I am right in saying that if I died after an act of contrition so perfect, realised while thinking of all of my faults, imperfections, omissions, etc., my soul would be absolved by God himself. Immediately afterwards, I fear that this was a proud thought. I pray to Jesus to comfort me.

And He does so by giving me this prayer:

Jesus, infinite Mercy, who forgave Levi and called him to Yourself, forgive us our sins because we sorrowfully regret having offended You.

Jesus, infinite Mercy, who forgave Mary Magdalene and placed her with the holy women and believers, forgive us our sins because we sorrowfully regret having offended You.

Jesus, infinite Mercy, who forgave Zacchaeus and made a disciple of him, forgive us our sins because we sorrowfully regret having offended You.

Jesus, infinite Mercy, who forgave the adulteress by giving her the divine commandment to sin no more, forgive us our sins because we sorrowfully regret having offended You.

Jesus, infinite Mercy, who forgave the repentant robber and brought him with You to Paradise, forgive us our sins because we sorrowfully regret having offended You.

Jesus, infinite Mercy, who forgave Peter for having denied You, forgive us our sins of infidelity because we sorrowfully regret having offended You.

Jesus, infinite Mercy, who from the height of the Cross invoked the Father's pardon on your enemies and your executioners, obtain for us the pardon of the Father, whom we have so often offended in offending You, the Most Holy Word of the Father. Obtain for us his pardon because we sorrowfully regret having offended Him.

Jesus, infinite Mercy, who forgave the Apostles so much, to the point of obtaining the gift of the Holy Spirit for them from the Father, whom they had offended by refusing to love God above everything (You, O God incarnate, that they abandoned in their cowardliness) and their neighbor (You, the perfect Friend and Master), obtain the Holy Spirit's forgiveness for us for the sins we have committed against these two loves, because we sorrowfully regret having offended Love, the very essence of God.

Forgive us, Jesus—You, the Mirror of the Father; You, the Fruit of divine Love—all of the sins we have committed against the Father, against the Son, and against the Holy Spirit, because we sorrowfully regret having offended the Most Holy Trinity. You alone can remove the stains caused by our faults since You completely poured out your divine Blood in order to make our souls clean.

We want to love You, O Lord!

Come to the rescue of our weakness. Come to our rescue when we fall. Infuse your love into us so that You can live in us, install within us the Kingdom of God, cause us to become one with You, who form one sole totality with the Father and the Holy Spirit, who is One and Triune, our Beginning and our End, the Origin of all our good, both present and future.

Be the sole occupant within us, live within us with your Holy Spirit who is all love, and proceeds from God the Father and from Yourself. May our souls repeat your most subtle promptings so that each one of our visible actions be only the clothing over your real actions within us, those that remain hidden. And may this be the result of a complete fusion, and even more, as a result of the complete annihilation of the creature, so that You alone live in us.

O most holy and eternal Mover, live and act in us by directing each movement of our soul, our spirit, our heart and even our humanity, so that all that is ours may become active in serving You in love and with love. O God, You deserve all of our love, and You ask us to love You because in love is found the Law, and the one who is able to love You with his entire being, and love his neighbor as himself no longer sins, and possesses your Kingdom in this world and in the next.

Be the sole occupant within us, O Son of the Father, who with the Father and the Holy Spirit form the one and unique God. Be the sole occupant within us so that when the Father looks at us, He will see within us his Beloved Son, He will love us in You and for You, our divine Host, and make his home in us to feel that He is with You.

Be the sole occupant within us, O Word incarnate, who were conceived by the work of the eternal Love, and who have never been separated from Him. Be the sole occupant within us so that when our spirit begins praying to glorify the Most Adorable Triune Divinity, and to invoke Him in our necessities and our sorrows, the voice that rises up to the throne of God may be still that of the Holy Spirit, expressing perfect praise and appropriate entreaty to Him, each agreeable to the Lord.

I do not ask You, O Most Holy Love, to make me live a life of grace that is personal to me; rather, I ask You Yourself, You, Grace, to live within me, so that I may really live a life of Grace, and be transformed to the point of becoming a true Christ.

"Father, don't let us succumb to despair"

May 15, 1944.

Since Saturday, I have put myself through a special penance for the poor ones who are in despair. They have always inspired compassion in me, even before having been subjected to this terrible ordeal.... Because of that, each day for the rest of my life, I will give God a special offering for my "brothers in despair." So that God will remove them from the horrible spasm in which they writhe like enraged bodies in a scorching pyre, and give them his drops of dew, his peace, his faith, his hope, and his charity.

It's too horrible not to love You, my God, not to hope in You, not to believe in You, not to hear You any longer, O my God! No, don't do that to anyone.

Prevent Satan and the world from plunging men into despair. Fortify those spirits who are indigent, fortify them through mercy, so that they will not fall into despair.

Strike them with other chastisements if they are unworthy of your blessings. But not this one, not this torture, Heavenly Father!

"Jesus, prevent me from thinking of the past"

August 9, 1944.

In obedience, I want to not think, to not remember ... But that memory is in me, even without my being aware of it. And if the spirit doesn't want to receive it, it's the mind that brings it back. And if the latter rejects the memory, it's the heart that cries it out. And if, in order to prevent the outcry, this latter one is crushed, it's the flesh that howls it. Once we have lived through hell, it's impossible to forget it afterwards.... And I tell Jesus:

Prevent me from thinking, O my Master, O my Love. Keep my poor head between your dear hands so that I may become unable to see, unable to hear, unable to remember the past, the voices of the past, the things of the past, and so that I may also not see the shadows of the future.

Prevent me from thinking, prevent me from thinking, O my Jesus. Thought means having in my mouth again the bitter flavor of despair, of folly. Have mercy, O good Jesus!

And I lean on the heart of Mother, who since August 2 has been staying near me, loving Mother who doesn't impose Herself, but whom I find immediately when I search for Her as a refuge.

"Show Yourself to the whole world, O Jesus"

June 24, 1943.

Yesterday morning, I said this prayer:

O Jesus, why don't You show the whole world how handsome You are, divinely handsome and divinely good?

If men saw You the way I see You, they wouldn't be able to misunderstand your infinite Goodness, they wouldn't refuse to love You with a love that would make them become good.

Martha would like You to show your angry Face in order to frighten. On the contrary, I ask that You show your loving Face in order to conquer the entire world as You have conquered me.

And Jesus answered:

"It wouldn't help. Love is not understood. If I appeared like that, some would mock Me and others would flee. Haven't you acted that way yourself? For years you spent your time running away from Me. And yet, in your dreams and in your inspirations it was always with love that I showed Myself to you. Even so, for years you were frightened of my manifestations. When I came close to you, you acted like my ancient Servant and Prophet: you would hide your face so as to not see Me. I had to prepare you with an infinite patience. Even now, deep down, you are still afraid that all of this is not real. Imagine how those who don't have my peace, but diabolical warfare in their heart, would react."

"Lord, not to see You, but to love You"

July 14, 1944.

Lord, I don't ask You for the glory of visions; rather, I ask You for the grace to love You more and more all the time.

"Lord, keep me humble"

June 13, 1947.

A lesson on a concept from Proverbs, ch. 25, v. 27: "He who questions majesty will be crushed by the glory."

Lord, I thank you for having chosen my nothingness. I beg You to keep me as simple as an ignorant child, so that I can always remember your Majesty and contemplate it, without being pushed by the desire to scrutinize its powers, so that I won't be crushed by your Majesty, which is so good and patient with little children, but so severe with the proud who want to raise themselves up, and who want to search You more than is permitted by your Will.

Holy Father, keep me in your Light so that I understand what You want. Make me blind or stupid, poor in everything, rather than allow me to become like those who scrutinize your powers, for whom You have such a great aversion.

"Jesus, Mary, Joseph, may my home be yours"

December 28, 1944, (12:00 o'clock).

Jesus says:

"Write:

O most holy King, adorable Heart, O my Master and Lord, I beg You to be the King of this house which is mine. May your Heart, which is full of mercy, spread its blessings upon it and those dwelling in it. May your Knowledge instruct all the hearts living in it, in the science of Good, of your Good. May your Power be the only ruler; so that no thought, no action or human desire will ever come to replace those which have been decided by your Will. Beginning now, and for all of the years to come, we want only You to give orders, directions and advice here. We abandon ourselves to You, body and soul. We are yours, always yours, for the earth and on the earth, for heaven and in heaven.

And you, O Mary, most amiable Mother, Lily of the Holy Trinity, place in this house your smile and your perfume of grace, reunite our hearts to the shade of your purity, enclose it in the calyx of your maternal love, preserve us from hell and its cruel legions by holding us against Yourself, on your virginal breast and on your immaculate and pierced heart. O Mother and Queen, be our Mother and our Queen.

Joseph, loyal guardian of the two most holy Beings, watch over us, who want to belong to them. Hard working and attentive, lead us towards the paths of salvation, and grant us protection in the dangers of life.

Jesus, Mary, Joseph, by your constant presence, transform this dwelling into a house of Nazareth. Heart of Jesus, heart of Mary, heart of Joseph, give us your love and take ours. Save us now and at the hour of our death.

Amen.

You will say this prayer to reconsecrate your house, and you will have each room blessed. Remember, and tell those who are with you, that where We are there must be nothing else that could offend our holiness."

"Peace to the dear departed"

October 24, 1944.

...I write what Jesus tells me:

"Now the month consecrated to the departed is approaching. Pray for them like this:

O Jesus, who showed us through your glorious Resurrection what the eternal state of the sons of God will be, grant the holy resurrection to our dear Departed who died in your Grace, and also grant this grace to us at our own hour. By the Sacrifice of your Blood, by the tears of Mary, by the merits of all the Saints, open your Kingdom to the spirits of our Departed.

O Mother, You who saw your martyrdom cease at Easter's dawn before the Risen One, You, who knew at the moment of your glorious Assumption the joy of seeing your wait transformed into apotheosis, console us in our sorrow by delivering our dear ones from their pain on the other side of death, and pray for us, who await the moment of affectionate reunion with those we have lost.

O Saints and martyrs who exult in heaven, turn your pleading eyes towards God for our departed brothers who are suffering. Pray to the Eternal One for them, so you'll be able to tell them: 'See, peace opens for you.'

O very dear Departed, who are not lost but only separated, may our prayers be for us the kiss that we are missing. When, thanks to our suffrages, you are free to enter into Paradise with the Saints, protect us by loving us with your Love of Perfection, united to us by the invisible, active and loving Communion of Saints. This is an anticipation of the perfect reunion of the 'blessed' which, besides giving us the beatific vision of God, may allow us to find you again as we knew you here on earth, but made sublime by the glory of Paradise."

By doing a bit of counting, I notice that today is the day when we begin the Novena of petition for the souls of our dear Departed. Jesus thus dictated it to me so that I can use it not only during the month of November, but also while saying my Novena.

"My soul is thirsty for You, O my Beloved"

...I lived through a time during which I felt myself transported by love in such an intense way that I had the impression of living outside of myself, outside of my being, so poor and full of faults. A seraph had taken hold of me and was making me burn in his impulses of love. My heart felt so dilated in this incandescent flame that I was suffocating. To relieve this torment I sang songs with improvised tunes, with made up words. I even put into music the Canticle of our Brother Sun, and several poems by St. Theresa of the Child Jesus. I repeated sacred songs. I needed a safety valve so as not to explode.

The night of February 10 (1934) I wrote my *Song of Love.*

My soul thirsts for You, O my Beloved. How my soul is thirsty for You! And how it searches for You everywhere, driven by the anxiety of its love.

Oh! Where are You? Oh! Who will be able to comfort me in this feverish search for my Good?

I would like to speak of the love that agitates me and oppresses me, I would like to meet other hearts in which to pour the plenitude of the gentleness that swells my heart. But alas! The world is deaf and insensitive to the great voice of love!

For loving souls, this is one of the biggest crosses: to have the heart, the soul and the lips rendered incandescent by the presence of the Beloved, and to feel at the same time the spirit of indifference and of rejection that surrounds and binds them.

These souls always live in anxiety for You, Love, amongst men. Alone with You, the Alone. They are in a desert because men cannot understand them.

And so they turn towards You, towards You, who are so far away, and so present in the souls that adore, towards You, who is the only One who can understand them, and satisfy their hunger, which is so great.

Oh! Satisfy this limitless hunger Yourself, You, the Only One who can. Multiply Yourself, pour Yourself into them because they have turned towards You like searching mouths, like cups that wait to be filled.

Let them be submerged by the waves of your love, let them be burned by the ardor of your flame, let them be annihilated in the flashing of your might.

They only ask to be immolated by You on a spiritual fire that elevates them in martyrdom.

Come, my Beloved, come, don't make me wait. My soul thirsts for You!

My soul asks You for love, an ever greater blaze of love, and better nourished. This soul languishes for You; its grief increasing along with its love.

Yet, even if there are moments when it invokes your pity, because the flame that wounds its heart is too strong, even if it asks for a moment of respite because your love is too violent, it nevertheless cries to You: Come, come towards this one who adores You!

What flavor will this love have in heaven if it tastes so sweet here on earth?

What will our meeting with You be like if now the soul dissolves at your fleeting passage, notwithstanding the distance that separates us?

What will the knowledge of You be, eternal Love? What will perfect Love be, the eternal union with You, if my poor love as a creature is now so strong, so sweet, so deep?

My Beloved is mine, and I am his.

Oh! Don't seek to tear me away from Him, O creatures! Don't try to come between my Beloved and me. Even if He should abandon me and hide his face from me, I will not cease to wait for Him and love Him as much as ever.

I shall await in peace the end of my sorrow, turned towards Him like a flower towards the sun. And the instant of his return will only be sweeter, when He turns his smiling Face towards his slave.

Nothing on earth can turn me away from Him, because He is gentleness, He is goodness, He is light, He is warmth, He is life, He is comfort, He is beatitude. He is the sweet Jesus who has ravished my heart.

Through Him and in Him each torment becomes sweet. All anguish is calmed in Him. All weakness becomes strength thanks to Him.

My Beloved is He, the Love that I love is He!

You can well see, Father, that even after nine years I still repeat the same things. They are always the same things. They cannot change.

"Crucified Jesus, increase my love in sorrow. Let me obtain the help of the blessed Virgin, St. Joseph, my guardian Angel"

[Transcription of February 9, 1946.]

O my adored Lord, crucified for me, divine Martyr of our love, I beg You to make me joyfully desire suffering. Increase my love for You in proportion to my suffering. If the flames of charity completely drown my soul, the suffering will be sweet, and sweet also will be the death I accept out of love for You and your creatures. Heart of Jesus, always be my good and my love.

O Mary, my Mother, when the storm is at its strongest peak and the cross is at its most critical point, give me the gentleness of your smile. When the soul suffers its passion, give me the comfort of your caress. When death frightens me, give me your breast as a refuge, and your Mother's heart to assuage my grief. O my Mother, I confide my life and my last agony to You. Let me die in your arms so that I may awaken in Paradise.

O devout patriarch, St. Joseph, at the crucial moment of my last voyage, come to me to guide my soul to salvation. May your look banish the infernal tempter from me. May my soul find refuge in your arms, that sheltered and rocked my Savior, and may it dart from there to eternal Love. St. Joseph, at the time of my last battle be my shield, so that may die in Jesus.

O my guardian angel, whom God has wanted to give me in his goodness, forgive me if up until now my love for you has left something to be desired. From now on, help me to love you, and to honor your presence more and more. Be always near me, especially at the hour of my death, so that the Evil One will not be able to disturb the serenity of my death, so that I may remain faithful to my Christian faith, and exhale my last breath in complete submission to the eternal Will. O my angel, at the moment of my death, accompany me to Jesus.

February 21, 1934.

Offering

Acts of self-offering

February 9, 1946.

Our Lord tells me to transcribe my acts of self-offering....

I solemnly offered myself as a victim soul to compassionate Love the day of the Most Holy Trinity of the year 1925....

I had a certain fear of offering myself to Justice, while thinking of the words of St. Theresa of the Child Jesus, who said: "If you want to offer yourself to Justice you should tremble, but to offer yourself to merciful Love, no. He will treat you with mercy."

While I was looking for my answer between a "yes" and a "no", the day of the feast of the Sacred Heart of Jesus came up, in the month of June 1931. During the Mass... I had the mental vision and the mental awareness of all of the catastrophes that have tormented us during the last ten years. An apocalyptic contemplation. I was taken by such an anguish, with irrepressible tears, that I couldn't see anything any more. Nothing but the abyss into which the world is preparing to fall, and the necessity of using victim souls as support, to prevent or at least slow the course of this world towards the precipice....

Back at home I wrote my act of offering, the one that I later recited solemnly the day of the feast of the Precious Blood. Here it is:

Act of offering as a victim to Justice and Love.

O my God, beginning and end of all power, of all wisdom, of all good, O eternal and uncreated Love, O Holy Trinity, be blessed now and for ever, be loved and adored for all eternity.

Only a miserable sinner, I dare to lift my heart, my voice and my entire being towards You, blessed Trinity, and I dare offer You this nothing that I am, as a host of expiation and love, so that this love for You will spread and overrun the world, and that the Kingdom of Christ install itself in it by bringing peace to men, this peace that only

You can give. I offer myself for the souls that are turning towards You, source of living water that quenches all thirsts and gives eternal life. I offer myself for the coming of your kingdom, for the return of your peace, for the redemption of the souls of the people that I know and love, that I cherish most of all because of the bonds that unite me to them, and also for the redemption of the souls of persons that I don't know or who are hostile to me.

By the intercession of the Most Blessed Virgin Mary and of St. Joseph, I pray that this sacrifice that I offer You, O my God, may be received and accepted in spite of its pettiness. It's really all that I can give You, and I give it to You with joy for the conversion of souls, for peace in the world, for prosperity, tranquility, peace, and every other good for my country; for the triumph of the Church over her enemies, for the return to God of those nations that are now victims of schisms and the prey of Satan, for the perfection of the priesthood, for my own eternal salvation and that of my parents, for the salvation of all the souls that I have loved, instructed in your Law and oriented towards You.

If I were to compare the brightness of your power with the misery that is my own, I would be annihilated before your might. If I compared my nothingness and my guilt to your perfection, I would have to run away, unworthy of remaining in your presence. But I have confidence in You, since it pleases You, and I give You my entire being, with my past, my present, my future, my faults, my efforts to do good, my failings, my immense desires of love that draw me towards You and towards souls. I think that You are Love, Mercy, Goodness. You are the Father, the Brother, the Spouse of our souls. You are personified Charity, and You don't push anyone away from your loving Heart. I am thus certain that You will bend in pity over your little slave, to accept her offering, listen to her prayer and satisfy her desires.

Oh! I will remain at your feet as long as You like, while waiting for You to show me with your smile that You accept my offering. I will not be afraid of the wait, knowing very well that it's only a trial You are giving me to test my faith. Neither will I be afraid of my own nothingness because I cover myself with the merits of my Beloved, who dwells in me. To present You my prayer, O Eternal One, I take up the unutterable words of the Word I adore, the words of my Master and Redeemer: "Father, forgive men, for they don't know what they're doing. Forgive them by the merits of Jesus Christ, by the merits of Mary, the merits of the martyrs and those of the saints. *If new expiatory victims are needed to calm and satisfy your offended Justice, here I am, O Father. I am ready to allow myself to be immolated for peace between man and God, between man and man, for the coming of your Kingdom.*"

O my Beloved, your Heart bleeds, constantly wounded by this tide of faults that overflows the world. Your thirst for love increases each day that humanity goes further away from You. Oh! Take me as a victim to console your outraged love.

I would like to renew this offering every time a sin wounds You, each time a new offense is thrown against the Most Holy Trinity. I would like to be innocent and rich in merits to be able to console You even more. I would like to have with me multitudes of souls ready to offer themselves to your love, but I find myself again alone and poor, myself laden with sins. I don't find myself frightened by my incapacity, my wretchedness, and my solitude. I am the way You want me to be. That suffices for me and gives me the courage to offer myself to You. It's You that placed in my heart this ever more lively thirst for love and immolation. This tells me that You want me also to belong to You, poor and weak as I am, a veritable nothing who becomes lost before your immensity.

Aware of my littleness, I pray that You don't treat me as your spouse or your sister. You are the Master of heaven and of the earth, I am the speck of dust.... You are the King of kings, and I am the last of your subjects. I know that in a royal household there are the sovereign's closest friends who are allowed to live day by day with him in his intimacy, but there are also servants whose duty is only to obey. Knowing this, I desire to be treated by You like a servant, or even less, O my Beloved. I want to be a slave whose only aim is to serve her Master humbly and loyally.

I want to be the blind instrument used for the triumph of Merciful Love on earth, the humble servant who gives herself completely for the cause of her King. I want to be the creature who remains in the dust, at the feet of your throne, Lord, to cover with my song the blasphemous cries of sinners, and with my loyal love console your pierced Heart. I want to be this creature who, thanks to her obscure sacrifice, is capable of obtaining many souls.

You Yourself said, O my lovable Jesus, that there is no love greater than the one who gives his life for his friends. Behold, I come towards You, I offer myself to You, O my only and perfect Friend, so that your Kingdom will establish itself on the earth and in the hearts of men.

You have also said: "Once I am raised up I will attract all towards Myself." I also, by your example, want to be raised on the cross of your suffering, on your redemptive cross that most humans are terrified of. Crucified with You, for You, I want to make up for those who sin, to obey for those who revolt, to supplicate You for those who forget You. In a word, I want to live an impetus of perfect love, that brings all back towards You, that sees You in everything, that loves everything for You and in You, that accepts everything from You, my infinite Good.

O my Beloved, by the cross which I ask of You, by the life which I offer You, by the love to which I aspire, make of me the happy victim of your merciful Love. That I may live in it and by it. That I may act under its prompting. Let each one of my deeds and each of my words, my thoughts, and my actions bear the mark of your love. Let it be my shield and my purification, my joy and my martyrdom. Let it be the cause of an ever more intimate fusion with You, until the final merging, when the soul, liberated, will come towards You and will unite itself anew to You, to adore You and love You perfectly and happily for all eternity.

"O Lord, give me your passion; by the intercession of St. Francis"

Love was growing in the contemplation of my dying God. It grew to the point of giving me a physical suffering that reached its apogee on Good Friday (of 1934).... A few days before experiencing this martyrdom that was sweet beyond measure and cruel beyond measure, I had composed a prayer that I was saying after the one of St. Francis:

O my Lord Jesus, before my death I ask You to grant me two things:

The first, I would like to feel in my soul and in my body, in a measure that is possible for me, the pain that You, O gentle Jesus, experienced at the moment of your very cruel passion.

The second, I would like to feel in my heart, in a measure that is possible for me, the extraordinary love that You, Son of God, were inflamed with to the point of submitting voluntarily to such an extensive passion for us sinners.

The one which I addressed to the Seraphic Father, read thus:

O my father, St. Francis, by the love with which Christ loved you and you loved Him, give me, I pray, the suffering and love that you obtained for yourself through your prayers.

I don't ask for the visible glory of the stigmata, of which I am not worthy, but to participate intimately in the sorrows and love of Jesus and you, so that by your example I may die of love for God and for souls.

The good Lord gave me what I asked for....

"May suffering be blessed, may love be blessed"

...In 1934, on Good Friday, I was pierced with love while contemplating my Jesus on the cross. Once I was able to get up, I wrote this page which I recite often, especially in the hours of greatest suffering, or during the time of Lent:

He is the Man of sorrows, the Beloved of my heart. To resemble God I must suffer also.

Come then, come then to me, O sweet thorns, O dear nails! Strike me, strike me, because the spouse wants to adorn herself with the jewels of the King.

Look at his eyes, how they are weakened, how his lips are dried out on the cross, while He prays for this guilty humanity.

O my heart, do you hear the "voice" that, while sobbing, murmurs words of love?

How great his suffering is! He dies for us, and He forgives. He promises paradise. While looking down with his sweet face, He says: "I thirst!", and He waits for our pity.

"What care can I lavish on You to calm the extreme suffering of your blessed lips, of your wounded heart? How can I go about relieving your chest, O Redeemer?"

"By your loyal affection and the generous gift of your suffering."

Oh! Come, come to me, O sweet thorns, O dear nails! To me this crown, to me these blows, to me these nails on this hard wood! May the head of my Redeemer rest on my chest and on my heart. I want to wipe these tears with my affection and my love. I want to quench his fever and console his agony.

Blessed is the suffering that causes me to resemble You!

May the cross also be blessed because it raises me up to heaven!

Blessed be the love that gives wings to my suffering!

Blessed be the day that saw your eyes fall on me to seduce me! Even more blessed be the moment that consecrated me to You! Truly sublime is the torment that for your glory unites me to your cross and your suffering, O my God and Redeemer!

Oh! Come, come to me, O sweet thorns, O dear nails! To me this ornament! Sculpt within me the countenance of my King!

And you, hard wood of the cross covered with blood, come, O come! On earth I want nothing else to sustain me!

My Redeemer waits for me in the brilliant light of heaven, no longer languishing and moaning, but resplendent forever.

Consumed by my love, I will fly towards Him one day. His cross and his thorns will be my ornament.

In the brilliant rays of heaven, among the rejoicing angels, He will change into precious stones all of my sorrows and all of my torments.

May suffering be blessed, may the cross be blessed. And blessed be the love that will be fulfilled in heaven!

"I give You all of my nothing, Lord, in exchange for the plenty that You have given me!"

...I'm unable to remember who it was, whose lips an angel touched with fire taken from heaven, and rendered him insensitive to human tastes in order to render him able to perfectly understand the nourishment of the Word of God, and to celebrate his splendors. But I find that God Himself, taking the place of the angel, purified both my heart and my lips with the fire of his sorrow, in order to render them able to taste the things that surpass the earthly plane.

And I bless You, O holy Father, for this scorching fire, for the power of your cauterization, for your action towards me as a Doctor who destroys the parts that are invaded by destructive infections, in order to restore life.

I bless You for your Love, which has saved me against my will, for your patience, that waited for me, for your indestructible Compassion, that none of our refusals can break, nor any of our faults, and which had pity on me in such a great unlimited way.

I bless You for having evangelized me anew, for having transformed me in Yourself without delaying when I told You: "I want to belong to You!"

A life on my knees, arms raised toward heaven in a gesture of love and benediction—my entire life isn't enough to thank You for what You have given me—and all the suffering I've given You and that I continue to offer You, because in my weakness and my misery I can only give You my suffering; they are a small offering, a very insignificant mite, an even more insignificant restitution in comparison to all that You have given me.

But, O Lord, O good Master, O untiring Compassion, for this nothing that I give You, which is all that I possess that is truly mine, and that isn't superfluous because these are not superfluous things that I give You, but things that are essential to life on earth, things that all seek to conserve as their greatest treasure, because it is a matter of my health, of my life, of my sacrifice, of my suffering; for all of this, Holy Trinity, for all of this, O my Jesus, concede to others besides me, to an infinite number of others who are as guilty as I have been at other times, what You have granted me, so that, thanks to their conversion and to their love, they may gain heaven with You.

"Jesus, I am now living your Gethsemani"

...Praying for those who don't pray. What mission can render us more like Jesus and Mary than to live lives that have been nothing but prayer. Praying when we are fervent, praying when our felt fervor is dulled, praying with a single word when we are incapable of doing otherwise because of sickness or other obstacles. Praying with a simple sigh, with a look aimed at heaven, praying with tears falling from our cheeks, praying through our sobs.

I look at my Jesus, who attained the apogee of prayer when He was raised on his scaffold. And in these, my own hours of Gethsemani, during which I find myself so alone and crushed by solitude, I imitate the meditative silence of the Redeemer. The meditative silence has more rewards than a flood of mechanical prayers which are recited with an absent spirit.

I look at Jesus on the cross. He is right in front of me. Raised up, pale, pierced, the skin rendered livid by the blows and by the agony. He senses himself watched, and He raises his head, which was bent over his chest, under his bloody crown. He looks at me. Our eyes meet through a veil of tears. He teaches me to pray in these hours of passion, expiation. And I learn by looking at Him.

I follow his look that turns about over the world. A look of infinite compassion for all human miseries. I follow his look. After having gathered as in a sheaf the spectacle of all human miseries, this look turns towards heaven. With this expression of love, which is so unrivaled, He offers them to the love of the Father to obtain his assistance.

Sacrificial souls must live this way. Sow love, gather suffering, offer love and suffering to obtain mercy. And the mute dialogue of our glances continues.

"I am thirsty for souls."

"I am thirsty for You."

"After this hour, I will come. For the moment, you must remain alone. Accept with joy that I am looking at you and that I am teaching you."

"Jesus, I'm alone."

"I also am alone. Souls don't love Me."

"Jesus, I feel menaced by the estrangement that threatens to drown me."

"Don't be afraid. It won't".

"I have the impression of being uprooted from You."

"No. If our Father has retired into the depths of heaven, I am near you, and Love, the Paraclete, covers you with his shadow. Consider, O creature, that our Father—and I say "our" because I am your Brother—does Himself violence in not holding you against his heart. One day you will know what all of this suffering was for. Look over there: do you see the immense crowd of needy people who must have holocausts to be saved? Turn your eyes to heaven and look at what chastisements a single act of love can prevent. And smile, O my dear sister, my poor sister. What you are able to do, the angels themselves cannot do. You have been allowed to immolate yourself, to expiate, and to adore. The angels have only been allowed to adore."

"I am afraid of not being able to do my duty well."

"My merits, which are infinite, make good your imperfections. I do not ask you, my dear little victim, to be perfect. I only ask you to try to approach this perfection as closely as possible."

"Are you happy, Jesus?"

"I am happy, Mary. Your efforts dry my tears."

And so? What should I say? "Father, deliver me from this hour?" But it is just for this hour that I was born. All that's left for me to do is to live it in all of its austerity.

"Thank You, Lord, for the gift of suffering"

August 19, 1944.

Jesus says:

"Write:

I know, O Lord, that the days You make me cry more are the days You make me gain more. Thank You, therefore, for making me cry.

I know, O Lord, that the days You make me suffer more are the days You make me assuage the suffering of others more. Thank You, therefore, for making me suffer.

I know, O Lord, that the days You make me agonize more because You hide Yourself are the days You go to one of my brothers who is lost. Thank You, therefore, for my agony.

I know, O Lord, that the days You leave me all alone on the bitter billows of desolation, which already taste of the salt of despair, are the days I give You back a despairing brother. Thank You, therefore, for these bitter waves.

I know, O Lord, that the shadows that make me blind, the hunger that makes me languish, the thirst that makes me die for You, of You, have the purpose of giving You—Light, Source, Nourishment—back to those who are dying of all deaths. Thank You, therefore, for this hunger, and for this thirst.

I know, O Lord, that my spiritual deaths on your cross are resurrections for as many deaths to your cross. Thank You, therefore, for all of these spiritual deaths.

Because I believe, O Lord, that all You do to me is for my good, has a good thing as a goal, and is for the glory of God: the supreme Good.

Because I believe that I will again find the fruit of all this when I meet You, and seeing You will make me forget all of the sufferings I underwent.

Because I believe that my joy will be increased for each suffering accepted.

Because I believe that my joy will see its brightness raised by the names of those that I've saved with my sufferings.

Because I believe that for the 'victims' there is no Justice, but only Love.

Because I believe that our meeting will be a smile, a kiss, it will be your kiss, Jesus-Love, and that this kiss will make all trace of tears disappear.

Because I believe all of this, I thank You for my numberless thorns, and I love You with an unrestricted love.

You didn't give me Mary's part, which is the best one, but your part, the part that is yours, the perfect part: Suffering.

Thank You, Jesus.

This is what you must say, and not only with your lips, but with a spirit that is convinced of telling the truth. The One who is speaking to you is Truth. If I knew of a less painful way to prepare you for a beautiful eternity, I would have chosen it for you, because I love you; but it doesn't exist. I have thus granted it to you because of my infinite love...."

"Let me suffer on your Heart, Jesus"

June 7, 1943.

Take my tears tonight. There's nothing else left for me to give You in this night of suffering. I'm not even saying to You: "Relieve me of this pain." I only say: "May your will be done; but help me, Jesus."

Yes, help me, O my good Master. Don't let me go. All of the suffering that You want, Lord, but your presence always.

I know, I believe that this moral suffering certainly has its reason for being. I know, I hope it's useful somehow. I know that by suffering peacefully on your Heart that peace will live in me and the demon's hate will be powerless against it. Therefore I say: "Here I am, for your love, to do your Will."

Only this morning I was saying that my present happiness was preventing me from feeling the corrosiveness of human events. But tonight I felt the harsh flavor of present necessities, and I suffered greatly from them. Had I been alone in my suffering, my suffering would have been spasmodic. But, knowing full well that no human creature could have consoled me, I addressed myself to You with confidence.

You want these acts of faith and love in compensation for all those actions of love that are denied to You. And, right away, You give your reward to the generous soul, in the form of consolation.

Now I have learned. I come looking for refuge in You right away. I don't content myself with praying to You; I push my courage even further and I come into your arms. You are my God, but You are also my Brother and my

Spouse. So I can permit myself to not only pray to You but also to embrace You, so that I don't feel alone facing a future that everybody is worried about, and that in my case is even more difficult to face.

Hold me this way during the entire month, which is painful to the extreme. Hold me like this until my death, even if You don't talk, as long as I can remain on your Heart.

Remember your agony, Lord, and be the consoling angel for your little victim.

"Jesus, rest on my heart"

...I had offered myself as an expiatory victim. It was thus necessary that I live as an expiatory victim. Jesus didn't want to talk; He couldn't. He didn't want to, couldn't make me see that He was present and that He was helping me by simply being present. In spite of his apparent stillness and his apparent sleep, in the hour when the storm shook my little boat in a thousand directions, my love for Him remained intact. That's what made up my comfort.

While being alone, I loved Him with the maximum of confidence. I was telling Him:

You don't speak, You don't move within me, but I know that You are present in spite of everything. I know that You hear me and that You see me.

I will love You for two: for me and for You. It's me that will speak to fill the places left empty by your silence. It's me that will act while You remain immobile.

I have never loved You more, even if in this moment I am not receiving anything from You, nothing from a human point of view, nothing from a supernatural point of view.

I know that what You are not giving me now, for the moment, will be given to me in its entirety in heaven, deposited by You in the bank of heaven and returned a hundredfold, because You, O my Love, You are a banker of unrivaled generosity.

I was telling Him:

My poor Jesus! You are perhaps tired.

You knock on the door of so many hearts to enter in and give comfort to your fatigue. You, the divine Pilgrim, You have no place to lay your head. You delight in living in heaven but not as much as in living among the men that You have bought back at the cost of your suffering. And no one wants to take You in.

Their house is already full of worldly preoccupations. You are the unknown stranger. When we see You arrive, we quickly understand that You aren't bringing human riches or earthly honors. We then slam the door in your face or even, what is worse, chase You off while threatening You with sticks or setting the dogs on You. And You are tired.

You have found shelter in a poor heart that is completely open to receive You, and You have fallen asleep with your sorrow in the heart.

Sleep, Jesus. Sleep offers a respite from our suffering. Sleep and rest Yourself.

While I travel around for You, looking for hearts, saying who You are, remain as Master of my house, the house of my poor heart.

O my Love, be at ease. I will make as little noise as possible so as not to wake You. If something hurts me, not a moan will leave my mouth.

I am contented in serving You by working for You, in loving You without You stopping me, in contemplating your divine beauty while You sleep in my heart.

I have never loved Jesus in a more supernatural way than when He wasn't tangibly reciprocating my love.

"Lord, I offer myself for Italy"

October 9, 1943.

Jesus says:

" ...O daughter of my love, it is necessary to pray much, much, much. I can't ask the sacrifice of other affections from you because you are as naked as I was while on the cross; but if it were possible, I would ask you for many more for this intention. I would help you; but in order to wash Italy, which is covered with mud, I need tears. I advise you that your sorrow will be acute in order to buy back many deaths, and to obtain for your country, Italy, many pardons on the part of God. Say with Me:

Lord, to preserve Italy from new catastrophes, especially spiritual ones, I agree to drink from the chalice of suffering. Stay with me, Lord, while my passion as a small redeemer is consummated.

I will always remain with you, up until the moment when I lead you to where the Passion ends, and where the glorious Resurrection in Me begins."

"I would like to have a thousand lives so that I could offer them all to You, O Lord"

All human reflection has fallen. Words and thoughts swim in the divine. And the divine doesn't know agitation, or nervouness, or exultation. It is Peace. A peace that nothing can upset. And my soul finds itself immersed in it.

I attained this shore after much suffering.

If it's really suffering that has served as an oar and sail to make me arrive more quickly with You, O God, who is Peace, Mercy, Love, may this Suffering be blessed once again.

If it's really through suffering that I, "nothing", have become "something" in your eyes, O God, may your Name be blessed again for the Suffering that You have given me like the most beautiful of gifts.

My soul praises You, O Lord. It exults in You, Who have wanted to look with benevolence towards this "nothing" that I am, to make it an instrument of good for other "nothings" like myself.

May your Name be blessed, O my Lord and Savior. You have delivered me from all of my enemies and You have covered me with your mercy. You have nourished me with your love. You have sustained me, forgiven me, instructed me and consoled me. You have become my Friend and my Parent, my Teacher and my Doctor.

You have allowed me to know You for the one You really are, the only true God, and to know the one You have sent: Jesus Christ. For this grace I would like to say "thank You" with each beat of my heart and for all eternity.

It still wouldn't be enough because the act of knowing You and loving You, O God, is such a great good that nothing can repay it.

You have permitted me to speak about You to the numerous beings that You have entrusted to me. For this also I say: "Thank You, my God."

For all of these beings, for those that I have loved, known, guided, and who have familial bonds with me or simply the bonds of human fraternity, I have prayed and suffered, O God, so that they also could enter in where, through your mercy, I myself have the hope of entering: your eternal Kingdom.

Even now, on the eve of my death, I pray for them, and one more time I offer You my life. Preserve them, O Father, from the danger of losing You, who are the Only True Good.

I pray for them, Lord, and for all of the poor souls who no longer know where the safe Road is, the true Life, the Light that never goes out.

Oh! Lord and Holy Father, I would like to have a thousand lives and another thousand, to offer them all like a sheaf of holocausts for the good of the world.

You can well see, O my Father and my God, that this cry gushes up from the bottom of my soul, and like the perfume of incense, rises like an arrow all the way to the foot of your Throne.

O Lord, don't look on the baseness of your servant. Look instead on the desire she has to love You. Look at the generous gift of her suffering, given to You so that good may take root in hearts that have become sterile.

Multiply the beats of my heart, and to each beat add one suffering. With the suffering, add the capacity to suffer. I ask You for this grace, O Holy Father, because You are the only One who can give it to us poor creatures.

And for my secret sacrifice of every moment, O Father, give me a multitude of souls that I can offer You.

Make them, as well as myself, walk in the light, in your light. O God, when time is over for us, open the gates of your Kingdom for us, and the gates of your Heart, so that for all eternity we can rejoice in You, O omnipotent God, eternal and trine.

Meditation

One hour with Jesus

June 14, 1944.

Jesus' Holy Hour.

I.

"If I do not wash you, you will have no part in my Kingdom."

You, soul that I love, and all of you that I love, listen. I am speaking to you because I want to spend this hour with you.

I, Jesus, do not distance you from my altar even if you approach it with a sick soul covered in sores, or enslaved by passions; these same passions that, like vines, bind up your soul and hamper you spiritually in order to deliver you, thus imprisoned, to the power of the flesh and its king, Lucifer.

It's always Me, Jesus, the Rabbi of Galilee, the one to whom the lepers, the paralytics, the blind, the possessed, the epileptics cried out in loud voices: "Son of David, have pity on me." It's always Me, Jesus, the Rabbi who offers his hand to the one who is drowning, and tells him: "Why do you doubt Me?" It's always Me, Jesus, the Rabbi who tells the dead: "Rise and live. I want it. Come out of your death sleep, come out of your tomb and walk," and I return you to the ones who love you.

And who is it who loves you, O my loved ones? Who loves you with true love, love that is not egotistical, love that is not changeable? Who loves you with an unselfish love, not stingy, and whose goal is to give you what he has accumulated for you, while telling you: "Take it. It's yours. I've done all of this for you so that this can be yours and you can profit from it"? Who? The eternal God. And Me, it's to Him that I bring you. To Him who loves you.

I don't distance you from my altar, because this altar is my flesh, my throne, the dwelling place of the Doctor who cures you of all disease. From here, I teach you to be confident. From here, King of life, I give you life. From here I bend over your illnesses and I cure them with the breath of my love.

I do even more, O children. I come down from this altar and I come towards you. See Me appear at the door of the churches. Few are those who enter them, and even less numerous are those who enter with sure faith. Here I am. Like a figure of peace, I show Myself in your streets, where you pass by overburdened, poisoned, withered by pain, by selfishness, by hatred. I offer you my hands. I can well see that you stagger with fatigue under the enormous stones that you have taken up and that have taken the place of the cross that I had put in your hand to sustain you as the staff supports the pilgrim. See how I tell you: "Enter. Rest. Drink," because I can clearly see that you are exhausted, parched.

But you don't see Me. You pass right by Me, you jostle Me, sometimes by ill will, sometimes from lack of spiritual vision. Sometimes you don't look at Me at all. But you know you are soiled, and you don't dare approach the candor of my divine Host. But this Candor knows how to be indulgent to you. Learn to know Me, men who distrust Me, because you don't know Me.

Listen. I wanted to leave the Liberty and Purity which forms the atmosphere of heaven and to descend into this prison of yours, into this polluted air, to help you, *because I love you*. I did more than that: I deprived Myself of my divine liberty and I became enslaved to a mortal flesh. The Spirit of God enclosed in a body, the Infinite closed up in a bundle of muscles and bones, submissive to the voices of this flesh, persecuted by cold and by the sun, by famine, thirst, fatigue. I could have ignored all of that. I wanted to know the tortures of man torn from his throne of innocence. I did that in order to *love you more*.

That still wasn't enough for Me. I wanted—because to be indulgent it is necessary to know what those we treat with indulgence endure—I wanted to experience the assaults on all of your senses in order to know your struggles, understand what kind of underhanded tyranny Satan slides into your blood, understand how easy it is to be hypnotized by this Serpent if we lower, for only a moment, our eyes into his seductive glance, by forgetting to live in the light. The serpent does not live in the light. He hides himself in dim nooks that appear restful but are dangerous. For you the dark recesses are named: women, money, power, egotism, ambition, sensuality. They hide the light that is God from you. In these dark recesses hides Satan. He looks like a necklace, but that's the rope that will strangle you. I wanted to know all of that *because I love you*.

This still wasn't enough for Me. It would have sufficed, but the Justice of the Father would have been able to say to his Flesh: "You knew how to avoid the snare. Man, flesh like You, actually doesn't know how to avoid it. Let him be punished because I can't forgive someone who is soiled." I took upon Myself your stains. Those of the past, those of the present, and those to come. I went beyond the experience of the prophet Job and, more than him, I was submerged in sin's putrid and rotten manure. This happened when, submerged by the sin of the entire world, I didn't dare to raise my eyes to heaven. I groaned under the weight of the anger of God the Father, anger accumulated over the ages, anger conscious of sins yet to come. A deluge of sins on the earth from its beginning to its end. A deluge of curses on the Guilty One. On the Host of Sin.

Oh, men! I was more innocent than the baby a mother kisses after his baptism. And the Most High, on seeing Me, was horrified, because I had become sin. I took upon

Myself all of the sin of the world. I perspired from disgust. I perspired my own blood because of the disgust caused by this leprosy that I had on Myself who am the Innocent One. The blood caused my veins to burst because of the disgust provoked by this fetid swamp that was covering Me. And to achieve this torture, to press even more of my blood from my heart, to these sufferings were added the bitter pain of the curse. In this hour I was no longer the Word of God: I was the Man. The Man. The Guilty One.

Is it possible I could not understand your dejection and cease to love you because you are dejected? On the contrary, *that is why I love you*. I have only to remember that hour to love you and call you "Brothers!" But that is not enough to make the Father call you "Sons," and I want Him to call you that. What sort of brother would I be for you if I didn't want you to also be in the paternal Home?

Therefore I tell you: "Come, so that I can wash you." No one is too dirty, to the point of not being able to be washed by my bath. No one is too clean, to the point of not needing my water. Come. My water isn't ordinary water. There are miraculous sources that heal sores and sicknesses of the flesh. This water is like that because it gushes from my bosom.

Behold the ruptured Heart that gives water that washes and purifies. My Blood is the clearest and cleanest water in creation. With its power it can erase all infirmity and all imperfection. Your soul becomes white again, clean, fit for the Kingdom.

Come. Let Me tell you: "I forgive you!" Open your heart to Me. In it are the roots of all your pain. Let Me penetrate it. Permit Me to undo your bandages. Do your sores disgust you? Lit by my light, they appear to you just the way they are: a swarm of disgusting worms. Don't look at them. Let Me do it. I have a light hand. You will only perceive a caress...and all will be healed. A kiss, a tear... and all will be purified.

Oh, how beautiful you will then be around my altar! Angels among the angels of the Ciborium. My heart will be in the greatest joy. I am the Savior and I scorn no one. I am also the Lamb who loves to wander among the lilies, and loves to let Himself become inebriated by their candor. It is to give this candor back to you that I became incarnate, and that I allowed Myself to be immolated.

Oh, I see how the Father smiles at you and how the Spirit of Love inundates you with his splendors, since the dirt of sin is gone from you.

Come to the source of the Savior. May my Blood pour upon the contrite soul. Let one voice, the reflection of Mine, pronounce these words: "I absolve you in the name of the Father, and of the Son, and of the Holy Spirit!"

II.

"One among you will betray Me."

One among you! Yes, in a proportion of one to twelve, one of you betrays Me.

Each betrayal is more painful than being pierced by a lance. Look at the Humanity of your Redeemer. From head to feet, you can only see wounds. Flagellation makes those who imagine it shake and those who undergo it agonize. But this tortured Me for only one hour. You who betray Me flagellate my Heart and have been doing so for centuries.

I have loved you. I do love you. I understand you. I forgive you. I purify you by using all of my Blood for this purifying cleansing. And you betray Me.

I am the Word of God. In heaven, I am glorious. But I'm not only in this heaven as a spirit. I am also here as Flesh. The flesh has feelings and affections. Why do you want to renew for Me, continually, that gnawing fire which is the presence of a traitor? Is heaven far away? No, my son who betrays Me. I am near you. *I am among you*. And you burn Me with the fire of your betrayal.

I look around, among the different classes of people, seeking comfort. In each one I meet gazes, but gazes of betrayal. Why do you betray Me? I remain among you so that I can do good for you. Why do you want to do evil to Me? I bring you my gifts. Why do you launch venomous snakes against Me? I call you: "My friends." Why do you answer Me: "Accursed?" What have I done to you? Do you know a man who is more patient than I am?

Look. When you are happy, no one abandons you. But if you cry, if your wealth disappears, if a disease makes you contagious, see that everyone backs away. I stay. More than that, I bring you even closer, since it is only then that you actually come. You no longer have anyone with whom to cry and talk, and that's when I remind you of Myself. I don't tell you: "Go away, I don't know you." I could say it, because, in fact, when you were rich, healthy and happy, you never came to tell me: "I am such, and I thank You."

But no. I don't claim even that on the part of one who isn't a giant of love. I do not claim the "thank you." It would suffice for Me to hear: "I am happy." To hear it from your mouth. To not be a stranger to your world. To know that you remember that I also exist. To know that you think of Me from time to time. It is Me who would say the "thank you" to God for you: my Father and yours. But see, you never come. I could say: "I don't know you." Instead of that, notice that I open my arms to you and tell you: "Come, we will cry together."

Look. *I am in the prisons*, in the tiny and degrading cells, sitting on the same seat as the convict. I speak to him of a liberty that is more real than the one that is found outside of these four walls, of a liberty that no longer fears being lessened by punishable faults. This convict is nevertheless someone who betrayed Me, by betraying my law of love. Maybe he killed. Maybe he stole. But now he is calling Me. See Me at his side. The world hates him. I love him. I have called "friend" the one who was killing Me and stealing my life. I can call "friend" this unfortunate one who returns to Me.

I am near the sick like a flame of love. In their fever they know my caress; in their sweat my shroud; in their dullness, my arm upholding them; in their anguish, my word. And yet many have become ill because of a betrayal of my divine law. They served the flesh. And the flesh, like a crazy beast, lost its way. Now it is causing them to also lose their lives. In spite of that, see Me present as the only one who never tires of their pain. I wake with them, I suffer with them, I smile at their hopes. If the Father wills, I transform their hopes into realities. But if I see that the decree is that they die, behold that I take this brother who trembles in front of the mystery of death, and when he calls Me, I tell him: "Don't be afraid. You think that death is darkness: it is light. You think it's suffering: it is joy. Give Me your hand. I know death. I knew it before you. I know that it's a matter of an instant, and that God supernaturally helps in reducing the sensory so as to not overpower the soul going through this extreme struggle. Have confidence. Look at Me. Only Me.... There! You see? You have crossed over the threshold. Come with Me now to the Father. Don't fear that either. I am with you. The Father loves those that I love."

I am in the deserted house. Not long before, they were filled with joyful voices. Death passed through, or hardship. The survivor goes along by himself. Friends have run. Those who are loved are far away because of work, or else because of death. There is sunshine in the sky, but for the survivor everything is black. There is peace in the night air, but for the survivor, there is no rest. They have certainly betrayed Me in this house, by turning creatures into gods. They have loved in an idolatrous fashion and, in doing so, they have betrayed my law. But I come in, and I put a ray of light in the darkness. I put peace where there was a tempest. This survivor has called Me..., perhaps without thinking too much about it..., perhaps without really even wanting Me with him. But I come without delay.

Oh! That's all I ask for, to be with you. All memory of past mistakes falls when you call Me: "Jesus!"

But don't flagellate my Heart. It is already open and empty of all its blood. Do not poison its wound. To those who have understood my sorrow of betrayed love, I say: "One among you will betray Me, give Me your faithful love to comfort Me." And I say it to all. I say it to the beloved saints, as God. I say it to the beloved sinners, as Jesus. Yes, the sinners too, for whom I became *Jesus*, can dress this wound.

Are you Samaritans? I know it. But my parable speaks of a Samaritan with a gentle heart who dresses the wounds that were not touched by the sons of the Law who, pushed by the need to serve God, continued straight ahead. They didn't understand that God is better served by love than by exterior practices.

I am the Wounded One who languishes along your routes. *The robbers* have assailed Me and *plundered Me*. The robbers: those who profit unworthily of my sacrifice as God who makes himself flesh. They plunder Me: this means that with their heresies, they remove my attributes. They plunder the Truth that by its resplendent coat excites their covetousness. Don't they know, the wretches, that this coat shines, yes, but because it is worn by the One who is the Sun? Don't they know that once it is in their hands, this coat becomes a common rag covered with the drool of their proud minds? The Truth is truth, and only when it is attached to God does it enlighten everything with its light. Separated from God, it becomes a language suited for the Tower of Babel. The Truth is both Science and Wisdom at the same time, but, apart from God, it becomes chaos.

You, even if you are Samaritans, nurse my wounds. Give Me your oil and your wine: *the oil*, love: *the wine*, the contrition of your self. Nurse my wounds. I have no disdain for you. May the sinner who washed and caressed my tired feet tell you if I disdain the sinner.

Never betray Me again. Go and sin no more. I forgive you if in all of you there is love for Me. Give Me a sincere kiss. I feel a burn there where my cheek was touched by the kiss of traitors. Nurse the wound on my cheek with a kiss of loyalty.

III.

"Love one another as I have loved you."

From the cradle all the way to the cross, from Bethlehem all the way to the Mount of Olives, I have loved you.

The cold and the misery of my first night in the world did not prevent Me from loving you with my spirit. Having been lessened, I, the Word, to the point of not being able to say to you "I love you" with my lips, I told you these words with my spirit, which is inseparable from that of the Father and works therewith in inexhaustible activity.

The agony of my last night on earth did not prevent Me from loving you. On the contrary, it touched the highest levels of love. It burned in the fiercest fire. It consumed all that was not love to the point of ejecting it all from my veins, along with my blood, the distaste for sin and the sorrow due to the abandonment of my Father.

Is there a love greater than the one that knows how to love even when it is hated? It is in this fashion that I have loved you.

The first gesture of my hands, a caress. The last, a benediction. At the center of these two gestures, where the first was born on a winter night and the last in the splendor of a beautiful summer morning, thirty-three years of gestures of love to express the same number of movements of love. Love in miracles, love in the caresses destined for children and for friends, master's love, benefactor's love, friend's love—love, love, love....

And love that is more than human, at the Last Supper. These hands that are mine, before being tied and pierced, washed the feet of the apostles, even the feet of the one whose heart I would have wanted to wash, and they had broken the Bread. With the Bread I also broke up my Heart. I was giving you that. I knew that very soon I would return to heaven, and I didn't want to leave you alone. I knew how easy it is for you to forget, and I wanted to give you the chance to see you sitting like brothers around the same table, my table, telling one another: "We are of Jesus!"

Is there a love greater than the one that knows how to love even its torturers? And yet it is quite in this fashion that I have loved you. And I was able to pray for you, as I died.

Love one another as I have loved you. Hatred strangles light. Even a simple grudge obfuscates peace. God is Peace, He is light, because He is love. But if you refuse to love as I Myself have loved, you will not be able to possess God.

As I have loved you. Therefore, without pride. This tabernacle which is before you, this cross which is mine, this Heart which is mine don't express anything but humility.

I am God, and I am your Servant. I stay here in the hope that you will say: "I am hungry" so that I can thus give Myself to you as Bread. I am God, and I show Myself to you naked and condemned on a piece of wood that at other times was a symbol of infamy. I am God and I beg you to love my Heart. *I beg you.* Through my love for you, because if you love Me you do good to yourself. I am God. With or without your love I am always God. But not you. Without my love, you are nothing: dust.

I want to have you with Me. I want to have you here. I want to make of your dust a light of beatitude. I want you to not die, but live because I am Life and I want you to have Life.

Love without selfishness. If you love with selfishness, it would be an impure love, destined to die in sickness. Love one another in a way where you wish others more good than you wish for yourselves. It's very difficult. I know. But, do you see this Eucharistic Bread? It has made martyrs. They were creatures like you: fearful, weak, even vicious sometimes. This Bread made heroes of them.

In the first part, I recommended my Heart for your purification. In this third part, to make saints of you, I am showing you this Table and this Bread of sinners. My Blood has transformed you into just men, my Bread will transform just men into saints. A bath washes everything, but it doesn't nourish. It refreshes, it gives some substance, but it doesn't become flesh within flesh. On the other hand, nourishment becomes flesh and blood; it becomes a part of you. My Nourishment becomes a part of you.

Oh! Think! Look at a little child. Today he eats his bread and also tomorrow, and tomorrow, and again tomorrow. See him now become a man: tall, robust, handsome. Did his mother make him like that? No. His mother conceived him, carried him, gave birth to him, nourished him with her milk and loved him, loved him, loved him. But if the small boy had only received kisses, kisses and love alone, he would have died of starvation. The small boy becomes adult thanks to the nourishment he eats. The man is thus an adult thanks to the nourishment taken daily.

The same thing applies to your spiritual self. Nourish it with the true nourishment that comes from heaven and gives you the energies necessary for your growth in Grace. Strong and healthy virility is always an advantage. Observe the behavior of someone who is always sickly; observe how easily he becomes harsh, impatient, unpleasant. My nourishment will give you health. It will make you strong and virile in spirit. You will be able to love others more than yourselves, as I did with you.

See, my children, how much I have loved you. Not only as one may love himself, but even more. To the point that I agreed to die in your place, to save you from death. If you love like that, you will know God.

Do you know what it is to know God? It signifies savoring true Joy, true Peace, true Friendship. Oh, the Friendship, the Peace, the Joy of God! It's the reward promised to the blessed. But it is already given to the one who, on earth, knows how to love with his entire being.

When it is authentic, love is not made only of words. It is also made of actions. Love is active as its source, who is God, is active. Love never tires of being active, even when the behavior of brothers engenders deception. Woe to him who, crashing into an obstacle, falls like a bird with wings that are too weak.

Even wounded, *true Love* rises. If it can no longer *fly*, it uses its claws and its beak, but it climbs. It doesn't want to remain in the dark and the cold. It wants to be in contact with the sun, a remedy for all ills. As soon as it finds itself reinvigorated, it takes wing again. It shuttles between God and the brothers, and between the brothers and God, like an angelic butterfly that transports pollen from the heavenly gardens to terrestrial flowers to fecundate them and brings to God the collected perfumes of the flowers, even the most humble ones, for God to take them and bless them.

But woe to him who goes away from the sun. *The Sun is my Eucharist.* In It, the Father blesses you, the Holy Spirit loves you, while I, the Word, act.

Come, take and eat. This is the nourishment that I recommend for consumption.

IV.

"If you live in Me and my Doctrine lives in you, you will receive whatever you ask for."

I descend into you and I become your nourishment. But, being the Center that I am, I attract you towards Myself. You nourish yourselves with Me, but for a greater reason I nourish Myself with you. Our two appetites are insatiable and continuous. The vine nourishes the buds. The buds shape the vine. Water swells the oceans, but it is the oceans that give water by evaporating into clouds and descending again in the form of rain. That is why you must remain in Me, as I remain in you. Our separation would bring death, not my death, but yours.

I am nourishment for the spirit and nourishment for the mind. The spirit nourishes itself on the Flesh of a God. All that is an emanation of God can only receive nourishment from God, who is the mold that formed it. Your mind nourishes itself on my Word, which is the Thought of God.

Your own mind! Intelligence is what makes you resemble to God. In intelligence, there is memory, understanding, and also will. As in the spirit there is a resemblance to God in being a free and immortal spirit.

Your own mind must be nourished by my Doctrine, to be capable of memory, understanding, and will for what is good. My Doctrine reminds you of the kindnesses and the works of God, it reminds you who God is, and what you owe Him. It causes you to understand goodness, and to discern evil. It gives you the will to do good. Without my doctrine you become slaves of other doctrines that carry the name of "doctrine," but are only fables, and, like ships deprived of their rudders and without a compass, you head for a shipwreck. You go off the pre-established course. How, then, can you say: "God abandoned me" if it's you who abandoned God?

Remain in Me. If you do not remain in Me, it means that you hate Me. And my Father will give the same back to you because whoever hates Me, hates the Father, since the Father and I make only one God. Remain in Me. Act in such a way that the Father will not be able to make the distinction between the tree and its branch, because of the sap that unites them and permits them to form one inseparable being. Act so that the Father can't determine where I end and where you begin, we are so much alike. Whoever loves ends up by borrowing the expressions, the ways, the gestures of the person who is loved.

I want you to be replicas of Jesus. Because I want you to receive what you ask for, and thus not have to endure any refusals (grounded in Me, you will only ask for good things). I want you to receive the same as what you asked for, because the Father continually pours his treasures of love onto his Son. The one who is in the Son benefits from this continuous outpouring without limit, who is Divine Love that rejoices in his Word and circulates in Him. Now I am the Body and you are the members of the Body. This signifies that the Joy that covers Me and comes from the Father, the Power, the Peace, and all other perfection that circulates in my veins, pours into you, my faithful who have become an inseparable part of Myself, here and in the hereafter.

Come and ask. Don't be afraid to ask. You can ask everything because God can give everything. Ask for yourselves and ask for others. I have shown you how to do it. Ask for those who are present, and for those who are absent. Ask for those who have already passed away, those who are alive now, and those who have yet to be born. Ask for your present time and for your eternity which will come. Apply that to yourselves and to those you love.

Ask, ask, ask. For everything. For the good people so that God will bless them. For the bad so that God will convert them. Say with Me: "Father, forgive them." Ask: health, peace in families, peace in the world, peace for eternity. Ask for sanctity. Yes, also that. God is Holy and He is Father. At the same time as you ask Him for the life that sustains you, ask Him for sanctity. Ask for all of his graces through the Force that emanates from Him.

Don't be afraid to ask. The bread of each day, and the blessing of each day. You are not solely matter, and you are not yet solely spirit. Ask for the former and for the latter, and you will receive.

Don't be afraid of going too far. For you, I have asked that we partake of the same glory. More than that, I have given it to you, so that you will resemble Us, who love you, and so that the world will know that you are sons of God. Come. In this Heart, which is mine, lives your Father. Enter. So that He may recognize you and say: "Let us rejoice greatly in the heavens because I have regained a son that I loved."

"I wanted to satisfy your request," says Jesus. "It's always I who have been talking: I wanted to let my Eucharistic Voice speak. Receive it as a gift from Me. I bless you, and with you I bless all those who will listen to it."

The hour of Gethsemani

July 6, 1944.

Jesus says:

«You can clearly see, my soul, that I really had reason to say: "The knowledge of my agony in Gethsemani will not be understood and will be transformed into a scandal"?

People do not believe in the devil. Those who do don't believe that the devil was able to vex the Soul of Christ to the point of making Him sweat his own Blood. But you who have experienced a fragment of this temptation, you can understand.

Therefore, let's talk together.

You have asked Me: "How numerous are the agonies of Gethsemani that You give me?"

Oh! Really many! Not for the joy of tormenting you, but solely out of goodness. Goodness as a Master, and goodness as a Spouse. O my little spouse, I would not be able to place on your shoulders, in one blow, all the desolation that hit me that night, and which no one has been able to guess or to understand with the exception of my Mother and my angel. You would go insane, and you would die of it. And so, in order to allow you to taste of my entire meal, I give you a morsel here, and a morsel there. My hope is to obtain a maximum of compassion and of love for Myself, your Spouse who suffers, and the maximum of redemption for your brothers.

Now you see why I give you all of those hours from Gethsemani. If you put them all together, in the same way that one who is building a mosaic sees his design progress up to the final results, you too, by assembling in your mind the memories of the different stages, will see the true Agony of your Lord.

Think carefully about the degree to which I love you. The first time I only gave you the vision of my physical agitation. And you, just in seeing Me pace back and forth, raise my arms, wring my hands, cry and fall down in discouragement with an upset visage, you were so griefstricken as to die from it.

I showed you this visible torture several times, until the moment came when you were acquainted well enough with it to be able to endure it. And so, from time to time, I have unveiled my afflictions for you. *My afflictions*. Afflictions of man. All of man's passions came up in Me like irritated snakes, hissing their right to exist, and I had to strangle them one after another in order to be free to ascend Calvary.

The passions are not all bad. I have already explained that to you. I use this word in a philosophical sense and not with the meaning that you give it when you mix up sense and emotion. Of the good passions, your Jesus-Man had some, the same as the all-just do. But even the good passions can become hostile at certain times. They become hostile when they form a chain with their voices, an extremely hard steel chain, extremely powerful and solid to prevent us from accomplishing God's will.

To love life, which is a gift of God, is a duty; to the point that the one who voluntarily takes his own life is as guilty as one who kills, and even more so. So, the one who kills sins against charity towards his neighbor, but might have extenuating provocative circumstances blinding him, while the one who kills himself sins against himself and against God, who gave him life so that he could live it until his summoning. Killing yourself is like tearing the gift of God from yourself and throwing it back into his face, screaming a curse. The one who kills himself rejects the idea of having a Father, a Friend, a Being of goodness in which he can have faith. The one who kills himself rejects all dogma and all articles of faith. The one who kills himself rejects God. Life must be appreciated.

How must it be appreciated? By becoming its slaves? No. Life is a good friend. It is the friend of the other, the True, the *Great* Life. The *little* life on the earth, like a young serving girl, gives service to her patroness and brings her food. The great Life finally achieves the perfect age thanks to the care lavished on it by the little life.

It is this life in miniature, exactly, that procures for you the fancy clothes that you need in order to enter the Kingdom of the Life in grand scale. It's truly this life in miniature that fortifies you through the bitter bread soaked in the powerful vinegar of everyday things, and that helps you to become adults and perfect in order to take possession of the Life that will not know any ending. That is why this existence which is passed in the sorrow of exile deserves to be called "dear." It's the bank in whose bosom the fruits of eternal riches come to maturity.

Is it good? Praise the Lord for it! Is it full of sorrow? Say "thank you" to the Lord. Is it distressing beyond measure? Never say: "It's too much." Never say: "God is bad."

I have mentioned it several times: "Evil—and what are tribulations if not a consequence of evil?—evil does not come from God. It's man, evil man who causes suffering."

I have mentioned it several times: "God knows up to what point you can suffer. If He sees that your neighbor causes you an excessive grief, He intervenes not only by increasing your capacity to bear up but also with celestial consolations. If the hour has come He breaks the wicked, because the wicked don't have permission to torture their better neighbors beyond measure."

Life is "dear" in the honest satisfactions that it gives. God doesn't disapprove of them. He Himself created the necessity to work. As a punishment, but also for the relaxation of guilty man. Woe to you if you live in idleness! For ages the world would be an enormous asylum of madmen who are in the process of tearing each other up. You are already doing it, because unfortunately idleness has entered your lives. Honest fatigue is a relief to the spirit, bestowing joy and a peaceful rest.

Life is still more dear because of the holy affections with which it can be adorned. God does not disapprove of them. Could God, who is love, disapprove of honest love? Oh, the joy of being a son! The joy of being a father! Oh, the joy of finding a companion who gives birth to the children of our own blood and our own name, and also children for God! Oh, the joy of having a gentle sister, a good brother and sincere friends! No, God does not disapprove of these honest joys! Not at all.

It's He who put love on the earth, and not only on the earth, as in the case of work, punishment and relief for the guilty, but also and primarily in the earthly Paradise, as a foundation for the great joy of being sons of God. "It is not good for man to be alone," said He. Without a companion man would have lived as if he were in a desert, even if he was the king of creation. Greatly appreciated were the animals by man as their king, but far too inferior to a son of God. Infinitely good was God for his son, but far too superior to him. Man would have suffered from solitude, feeling himself too far removed from the world of divinity as well as from the world of the animals. It is for this reason that God gave him a companion.

Not only that. From the chaste love that man would have shared with his companion, God would have permitted the birth of the most gentle children, in order to give to the man and to the woman the possibility of pronouncing the sweetest word after the Name of God: "My son!"; and in order to give children the chance to pronounce the holiest word after the Name of God: "Mother!"

Mother. The one who says "mother" is already in prayer.

Saying "mother" signifies thanking God for his Providence that gives mothers to the children of men, and also to the wild animals' little ones, and to those of the domestic animals, to the young of the birds, and even to those of the silent fish, so that man will not know the horror of growing up alone, and not fall from lack of support, still being too young to know the difference between Good and Evil. Saying "mother" signifies blessing God who shows us the meaning of love through the kisses of our mother and the words of her lips. Saying "mother" signifies knowing God, who gives us a reflection of his principle attribute, Goodness, through the indulgence of our mother. And knowing God signifies hoping, believing and loving. It signifies attaining salvation.

The presence of a brother, couldn't it be compared to a plant placed next to another identical one, and capable of lending a strong hand during stormy times with its interlacing branches, and also capable, in springtime, of increasing the number of its flowers through exchanges of pollen?

That is why I have asked Christians to call one another "brothers." It suits you well since you have the same origin in God, and the same origin in your human blood. It's beneficial because it's sweet and comfortable for those who don't have a brother according to the flesh to be able to say to their neighbor: "My brother, I love you. Love me."

A sincere friend, isn't he like a travelling companion? Walking alone is too sad. When God grants a victim soul the grace of solitude, He makes Himself the travelling companion, because you cannot remain alone without weakening.

Life is like a steep road, rocky, often interrupted by crevasses and dangerous streams. The path is rendered even more dangerous by venomous snakes and thorny brambles that sting and tear. Being all alone would mean foundering. That is why God created friendship. When there are two of us, power and courage are augmented. Even heroes have moments of weakness. If a hero is alone, on whom will he be able to lean? On the thorny brambles? Who will he be able to cling to? To the venomous snakes? Where will he be able to stop? In the turbulence of the waters? In the darkness of the abyss? He would find a new danger everywhere. But now look at a friend. His chest is a place of rest, his arm a point of support, his affection a balm. And the hero regains his strength. The traveller sets back out on his travels heartened.

To give value to friendship I wanted to call my apostles friends. I so much appreciated their friendship that in the hour of my greatest agony I wanted them close to Me, on Gethsemani, the three dearest apostles. I begged them to wake with Me and to pray with Me, for Me.... Seeing that they were unable to do so augmented my sufferings and weakened Me to the point that I became more vulnerable to satanic seductions. One word. If I could have exchanged only a word with my friends, on the watch and capable of understanding my state, I would not have lost my blood before the Sacrifice, in the struggle to push Satan away.

But life and affections must not become adverse elements. Never. If they do become so, it is necessary to crush them.

And I crushed them. One after the other.

I had already mastered the humanly unbearable disgust provoked by the attitude of the Traitor. A nerve of my Heart was destroyed by this effort.

See that at this time the fear of losing life rose up. Life! I was thirty-three. In that hour I was *man*. I was the Man. So I had for life the same virgin love that Adam himself had for it in the earthly Paradise. The joy of being alive, of being healthy, of being strong, handsome, intelligent, loved, respected. The joy of seeing, hearing, and of being able to express Myself. The joy of breathing air that was pure and sweetly scented, the joy of hearing the music of the wind in the olive trees, that of the brook breaking over stones, that of the nightingale expressing its love in the manner of a flute. The joy of seeing the stars of the sky shine for Me like so many living torches, with love. The joy of seeing the earth become silver-colored again under the light of the moon, a light so white, so glistening, that we could have said that each night the earth became a virgin again, and that it was impossible for the Evil One to work under such a guileless veil of peace.

And I was destined to lose all of that. No more a question of seeing, of hearing, of moving. No more a question of being healthy, or of being respected. I would have to become the fetid carrion that we move out of our way with our foot as we turn our head in disgust; the miscarriage expelled by the society that was condemning Me, so that it could feel free to give itself to its sordid loves.

Friends! ...One of them had betrayed Me! And while I was awaiting death, he was hurrying to deliver it to Me. He thought he would be able to rejoice at my death.... The others were sleeping. And I loved them anyways. I could have awakened them, escaped with them, gone far, elsewhere, and saved my life and their friendship. Contrary to that, I had to remain, and be silent. Staying meant losing my friends and my life. Staying meant being rejected.

My Mother! Oh, love of my Mother! Love bent under my sorrow! I called you, and then pushed you away so that I wouldn't cause you to die from my sorrow! Oh, love of my Mother!

Yes, I know it, each one of my sobs reached you, O holy Woman. Each of my calls traversed space and penetrated like a spirit into the closed room where, as you always did, you were spending the night in prayer. That night, the prayer wasn't one of ecstasy, but one of torture for the soul. I know it. I was stopping Myself from calling you so that you wouldn't share the sorrowful cry of your Son, O martyr Mother, who was beginning your passion, surrounded in your solitude as I was in mine on the night of Holy Thursday.

The child who dies in the arms of his mother does not die: he falls asleep, rocked with kisses, kisses that the angels take up and continue until the moment when the sight of God removes from the child the desire for his mother. But I had to die on a cross, through the work of an executioner. I had to close my eyes for the last time and hear as a last thing shouts of malediction, menacing gestures.

How I loved you, O Mother, in this hour of Gethsemani!

All of the love that I had given you and that you had given me in thirty-three years was before Me. These thirty-three years of love and of life were there, and were pleading their case. They were pleading with Me to have pity on them, to not forget your kisses, your care, the milk you had given Me, the hollow of your warm hands on my cold little feet as a poor child, the songs of your lips, the lightness of your fingers on my curly hair, your smile, your look, your words, your silences, and your soft step of a dove that touches the ground with its feet but always keeps its wings ready for flight, and doesn't even crush a blade of grass, so light is its step. You were on the earth for my joy, Mother, but your wings were always ready to fly towards heaven. O holy, holy, holy and loving Mother!

All of the tears I had already cost you, those that were falling at that time from your cheeks, those that would yet fall during the next three days, know that I heard them fall like a rain of laments. Oh, the tears of my Mother!

Who can listen to his own mother cry without keeping for the rest of his days a tearing memory of those tears? I had to dissipate, strangle the human love that I had for you, Mother, and trample on your love and mine so that I could walk under the voice of the Will of God.

And I was alone. Alone! Alone! In heaven and on the earth there no longer was a single being for Me. I was the Man charged with the sins of the world. I was thus hated by God. I had to pay to redeem myself and to be loved again. I was the Man bringing the Goodness of Heaven. I was therefore hated by those men to whom Goodness is repugnant. I had to be killed because of my goodness, in punishment.

And you, too, honest joys of work accomplished in order to procure daily bread, and to give spiritual bread to men, you, too, honest joys, you presented yourselves before Me to tell Me: "Why are You leaving us?"

Nostalgia for the peaceful house, sanctified by so many pious prayers, become a Temple for receiving the nuptials of God, become heaven for having covered in its walls the Holy Trinity closed up in the soul of the Spirit of God!

Nostalgia for the humble and sincere crowds to whom I had given my light, to whom I gave my favors, and who thanked Me with love! Voices of children who called Me with a smile, voices of mothers who called Me with a sob, voices of the sick who called Me with a moan, voices of sinners who called Me with trembling! I could hear them all, and they were telling Me:

"Why are You abandoning us? Don't you want to caress us any more? Who will be able to caress the curls of our brown or blond hair as You do?"

"You no longer want to give us back our dead, heal our dying? Who else will have the same holy pity on mothers, O holy Son?"

"You no longer want to heal us? Who will heal us if You disappear?"

"You no longer want to save us? You are the only One who can. Every word from your mouth is a force that breaks a chain of sins in our somber heart. We are sicker than the lepers. For them, the illness ends when they die; for us it augments. If You leave, who will understand us? Who will treat us with justice and piety? Who will raise us back up? Stay with us Lord!"

"Stay! Stay! Stay with us!" cried the crowd of good people.

"Oh Son!" cried my Mother.

"Save Yourself!" cried life.

I had to crush these throats that cried. I had to strangle them to stop them from howling, to be able to have the strength to break my own heart by tearing out one of its nerves after another so that I could accomplish the Will of God.

And I was alone. That is to say, alone with Satan.

The first part of the temptation had been painful, but I was still able to feel the eye of God and hope in the love of my friends.

The second was more painful because God was withdrawing and my friends were sleeping. They confirmed the suggestion whistled by Satan, and sung by life: "You are sacrificing Yourself for nothing. Men won't love You more for your sacrifice. Men don't understand."

The third..., the third temptation was madness, despair, agony, death. The death of my soul. At my resurrection, my body alone did not resurrect. My soul also had to be resurrected because it had known death.

This should not look like a heresy to you. What is the death of a soul? It is eternal separation from God. And so: I was separated from God. My soul was dead. It is the true hour of eternity that I leave to my beloved ones, such as yourself, my little spouse, to seek to identify since you've been told that your lot is like that of Veronica Giuliani, who at the end of her life knew this tearing, more intense than all superhuman pain.

Us, we know the death of the spirit without deserving it, in order to understand the horror of damnation, the torment of impenitent sinners. We know it in order to save them. It breaks the heart, I know. Sanity see-saws. I know all of that, my dearly beloved. I lived it before you did. It is the infernal horror. We are at the mercy of the Demon because we are separated from God.

Do you think that Martha, who conquered the dragon, trembled more than us? No. The suffering is greater in us. The ferocious beast conquered by Martha really was a ferocious beast, but it was an earthly beast. We, we are prevailing over the Beast-Lucifer. Oh! There is no comparison! And the Beast-Lucifer approaches us more when heaven and earth distance themselves.

I had already been tempted in the desert. A temptation of reduced proportions, because in the desert the only weakness I had was due to the lack of material nourishment. On Gethsemani I was as starved for spiritual nourishment as I was for moral nourishment, and there wasn't any bread to nourish my Spirit, nor my Heart. God was no longer there for my Spirit, and tender affections were no longer there for my Heart.

See then appear, subtle as a breath of wind, penetrating as the sting of a bee, irritating like the poison of a viper, the voice of Lucifer. A flute that sounds on the sly , in a way so gentle and so soft that our attention is not awakened. It penetrates us with the seduction of its magic harmony, and it puts us to sleep. We would believe it to be a balm, a nearly spiritual medicine.

Oh eternal liar, how subtle you are! The ego asks only to be helped, and we would say that this melody is only there for that. Words of compassion and understanding, soft like the caresses on a forehead burning with fever, relieving like an ointment on a burn, dizzying like good wine poured into an empty stomach. And there, the tired soul falls asleep.

If the soul wasn't ultra vigilant with its subconscious, which is really alert only in those who have developed the habit of remaining united to the Love, it would end by falling into a lethargy that would place it entirely in Satan's power, in a hypnotic slumber in which Satan would be able to make it do anything. But the soul that has nourished itself constantly with Love doesn't lose the control of its subconscious, even when men and God seem to work together to make it see-saw in insanity. The subconscious wakes the soul. It cries out: "React! Wake up! Satan is behind your back!"

A terrible struggle begins. The poison is already in us. We must therefore resist, in spite of its effects, against the ever more violent and increasingly frequent waves of new poison that Satan spills into us with his suggestions.

The din increases. It is no longer the sound of the muted flute. It is no longer a caress or an ointment. It is the uproar of several instruments in high resonance. It is the striking of a club. It is a stab wound. It is a burn from a suffocating flame. And in this flame we see our lives unfurling before the eyes of our spirit. It had already passed away with a resigned aspect from things sacrificed. Now it is back dressed like an all powerful queen, and says: "Worship me! I am the one who makes the rules! Look at my gifts. Look at those I've given you, and look at those I will give you if you swear fidelity to me."

And in the sound of these instruments, the voices of things and people return. They are no longer content to pray. They order, they throw accusations, they insult, they curse, because we abandoned them. All comes back to torment us. *All.* And the disoriented soul struggles in an increasingly more feeble way.

While the soul vacillates and staggers like a warrior drained of his blood, while it looks for support from heaven or from earth so as to not give in, that is when Lucifer offers his shoulder. There is only him.... We call for help....

There is no response besides his.... We search for a compassionate glance.... We find none but his....

Woe to him who gives in to the illusion that Satan can be sincere! With all that is left of our energy we must distance ourselves from this artificial support, we must go back into solitude, close our eyes, and contemplate the horror of our destination rather than the false image that was proposed to us. We must raise our trembling hands and cover our ears with them to prevent the deceitful voice from entering them.

By acting this way all weapons fall. We are no more than a poor dying thing, alone. We no longer even succeed at praying with words because the acidity of satanic breath squeezes our throat. Only the subconscious prays. It prays. It prays. As a pinned butterfly continues to beat its wings in its agony, so our subconscious beats its wings, to say with each stroke: "I believe, I hope, I love. I believe in spite of everything. I hope in spite of everything. I love You in spite of everything."

He doesn't say: "God." He no longer dares to pronounce his Name. He feels himself to be too dirty because of the presence of Satan. But this Name is traced by the bloody tears of the heart on the angelical wings of your spirit, which you call subconscious, while in reality it is the superconscious. With every wing beat this Name shines like a ruby struck by the sun. God sees it, and the tears of his divine pity surround with pearls the rubies of your blood which fall in heroic drops....

Oh! souls who rise to God with this Name thus written with rubies and pearls...! Flowers in my Paradise.

Satan was telling Me, because his voice penetrated in spite of everything: "You see. You are not yet dead and they have already abandoned You. You see. God Himself is not coming to your rescue. If God, whose Son You are, doesn't love You, can You ever hope for man to be grateful to You for your sacrifice?

Do You know what they need? Vengeance! Revenge Yourself, O Christ, on all these fools, on all these cruel spirits. Revenge Yourself, strike them with a miracle that will reduce them to dust. Show Yourself the way You are: God. The terrible God of Sinai. The terrible God who struck me down and who chased Adam out of Paradise.

Up until now You have spoken words of goodness. Your rare reproaches were too gentle for these wild beasts whose skin is thicker than the leather of hippopotamuses. Your glance covered Your words like a balm. You only know how to love. Learn to hate and You will reign. Under the rod, hatred keeps backs bent and passes triumphantly over these enslaved spines. It crushes them. And they are happy to be. They are nothing but sadists. Torture is the only caress they appreciate and remember.

Is it too late? No, it's not too late. Are soldiers already heading in this direction? It's of no importance. I know that You are preparing Yourself to be gentle. That's a mistake. In the past I taught You to triumph in life. You didn't want to listen to me, and you can well see that now You are a loser. Now listen to me. Listen to me now because I am teaching You to triumph over death.

Be King, and be God. You have no weapons? No soldiers? No wealth? I told you before that a bit of love, the bit that is left of my treasure of love that used to be my angelic life, remains in me for You, who are good. I love You. I love You, my Lord, and I want to serve You.

You are the Redeemer of men. Why don't You want to be so for your fallen angel? I was your favorite because I was the brightest one, and You are the Light. Now I am darkness. But the tears of my torment have filled hell with liquid fire, there have been so many. Let me redeem myself. Only a little while, may I become man. Man is always much inferior to the angels. But how superior he is to me, a demon!

Cause me to become a man. Give me the life of a tortured man, anguished as much as You want. That will always be a paradise in comparison to my demoniac torture. And I could live in a way to deserve thousands of years of expiation to finally achieve anew the Light: You.

Let me serve You in exchange for what I'm asking You. No weapon can defeat mine, no army is larger than mine. The wealth at my disposal is without limit and I would make You king of the world if You accept my help. All riches will be your submissive slaves. Look: your angels, the angels of your Father, they are absent. But my angels are ready to disguise themselves as angels of light to surround You like a crown, and astonish the ignorant and evil masses. You don't know how to pronounce imperious words? I will suggest them to You myself. That's what I'm here for. Speak loudly and menacingly. Listen to me. Say lying words, but triumph. Speak words of curses, and say that it's your Father who suggests them to You.

Do You want me to imitate the voice of the Eternal? I will do it. I can do everything. I am the king of the earth and of hell. You are only the King of Heaven. So I am greater than You. But I will put everything at your feet if You want it.

The Will of your Father? But how could You think that He wants the death of his Son? Do You think He can harbor illusions about the purpose of this death? You insult the intelligence of God.

With your holy Word You have already bought back those who were susceptible of redemption. You don't need to continue trying. Believe me: those who don't change because of your Word, won't change because of your Sacrifice. Your Father certainly wanted to test You. But your obedience is enough for Him. He doesn't want anything more.

Oh, how much more You could serve Him by staying alive! You could travel across the world, evangelize, cure, uplift. Oh happy destiny! The world lived in by God! Behold the true redemption: reconverting the earth into a terrestrial paradise, a paradise where humans live again in holy friendship with God, hears his voice and contemplates his appearance. A destiny even happier than that of the first Couple. Because they would see You: true God and true Man.

Death! Your death! To be torn away from your Mother! The contempt of the world! Why? Do You want to be faithful to God? Why? Is He faithful to You? No. Where are his angels? Where is his smile? What do You have as a soul now? A torn shred, wrinkled, abandoned. Decide. Tell me yes.

Do You hear? They're coming out of the Temple, the executioners. Decide. Free Yourself. Be worthy of your Nature.

You are a sacrilege because You permit hands dirtied from lewdness and blood to touch You: You the Saint of saints. You are the first sacrilege of the world. You give the Word of God to pigs. You put pearls in their mouths.

Decide. You know what sort of death awaits You. I am offering You life, joy. I am giving You back your Mother.

Poor Mother! She has no one but You. See how she agonizes..., and You are preparing Yourself to make her agonize even more. What sort of son are You? What kind of respect do You have for the law? You do not respect the God that You are. You don't respect the One who bore You.... Your Mother.... Your Mother.... Your Mother."

I answered.... Maria, I answered by gathering my strength, by drinking the tears and the blood that ran from my eyes and the pores of my skin, I answered:

"I no longer have a mother. I no longer have a life. I no longer have divinity. I no longer have a mission. I no longer have anything. *Except for doing the will of the Lord my God*. Back away, Satan! I have said it the first and second time. I repeat for the third time: "Father, if it's possible, remove this cup from Me. As long as your Will is done and not mine. Begone, Satan. I am of God."

Maria, this is how I answered, and my Heart was broken with the effort. The drops of blood that I was sweating became like streams. No importance. I won.

I vanquished death. I, not Satan. We can vanquish death by accepting it.

I had promised you a *great* gift. I have granted it to you as I have done only to a very few.

You have known the extreme temptation of your Jesus. I had already unveiled it for you. But you were not yet ripe enough to understand it fully. Now you can.

You can see that I have reason to say that it will be neither understood nor accepted by these little Christians who are not formed enough, and remain in the state of larvae who don't want to evolve. Go in peace.»

The Mother's hour of desolation

June 3, 1944, First Saturday, (1:30 AM).

Mary says:

« This is Mother. Write.

Every Saturday, meditate on the Mother's hour of desolation. Spend the night between Friday and Saturday like that. I thank you with a blessing.

The first and third points are easy for you. You are only rereading the visions and dictations that you've already received. But the second point is painful for you because you have to do it by yourself.

In your description you said: "Mary with her group... goes back to the house by the shortest route." If this is sufficient in the description—because physical weakness didn't allow you to go any further—it does not suffice for your present prayer.

So, for your direction, write what I suffered at that moment.

When the stone took its place closing the tomb, I believed it was rolling on my heart and was crushing it while tearing it from my chest. I threw myself against it with my nails and mouth, to push it back away. This stone was separating me from Jesus, it was killing me a second time with a more profound death, with an even greater separation which even kept me from the mortal remains of my Son.... But, alas! All of that was for nothing. My nails and my teeth passed over the rock without changing anything. My fingers and my lips bled, but the rock remained closed in an inexorable way, like death.

And along with the blood there flowed my tears. This blood and these maternal tears were the first to wet this holy site, where God knew death to remove man from his death.

They tore me from there, because I would have continued to cling to this stone if I had been allowed. I would have stayed there, at the foot of this door of stone, like a beggar who is waiting for a mite. In effect, I was the most miserable of women, and to live I needed this mite: to see my Son! I was still less than a beggar. I would have laid there like a lamb without a shepherd, lost, starved, alone, who returns to her sheep-pen, a pen without a master, and who lets herself die of hunger there, against the barrier, because she no longer has anyone, and because in a world full of wolves she has the impression that she is secure if she stays where there was once someone who loved her.... Wasn't I a lamb in the middle of ferocious wolves, and wasn't the One who loved me dead?

They tore me from there.... Oh, men! How cruel they are, sometimes, in their pity! What would these days have been for me, in the midst of the tranquil vegetation, awaiting the resurrection of my Jesus? Much, much less tearing than those I had to live elsewhere.

In this place there was no trace of murder. The plants, innocent and good, continued to flower to give glory to God. The birds, innocent and good, continued nesting and singing in obedience to their Lord. No hatred with them, no curses, no murder. Yes, they had heard the clamor of hatred and the blasphemies and they huddled up in the hollow of the branches while the trees shook in the wind of the storm. They had seen their Lord bruised, wounded, dying, pass by as if He also had been a bird chased by a falcon or by a pack of cruel children. They had pity, and ended up by also being afraid, thinking that if man kills the Creator, who is so good, it was also the end of all creation. The Creator had always had words of love, blessings, and crumbs of bread.

In this peace, I could have given my torment some respite. In this peace I could have cried without spasms under the stars and in the light of day, up til the moment when Easter Sunday's dawn would have opened the doors for me and returned my Son.

The guards? I was never really afraid of them! I would have huddled in a corner like a slave awaiting his master. They would have had such a pitiful and negligible image of me that they would have forgotten me. And even if they had mocked me, what would they have done to me? Of how many insults had I been the object on the summit of Golgotha? More atrocious words don't exist. I had drunk all the dregs of the most obscene human language. Since then, any blasphemy in my regard, *in my regard*, does not astonish me any more, no matter how atrocious it is. I would thus have been able to endure the jeers of a few half-asleep guards.

But I was torn from this place.... And I had to return among men. Men! Men! Ferocious beasts who had killed my Son. This was the second Calvary of the Mother....

Behold the route...! It still carries the signs of the ravages provoked by the torrent of people who traveled it that morning behind the Condemned One, and in the afternoon to escape far from that hill. To return to the house, I had to use a way that had been traveled by the cruel executioners. See the traces of their steps. The footsteps went in all directions, scraps of cloth, lost objects, as one finds where there has been a crowd, and in the confusion the men crush one against the other. Each of these traces, each of these signs was telling me: "I belong to one of your Son's executioners."

And now look at the *real* route of Calvary there, at the little bridge, outside of the gate.... Here the traces are more condensed, and my sorrow becomes again more atrocious.... Scattered on the ground I see stones and sticks.... I know what they were used for. Amongst them there are surely some that have traces of blood, the blood of my Child, because they wanted to hit Him on top of wounds that were already inflicted...! Oh! On these things which are not guilty, that man has rendered guilty, I would like to search for the Blood of my Son. But they don't let me.

Night is approaching. It's Friday, Friday before Passover. We need to hurry.

Before turning my back on Calvary to take the road that enters the town, I raise my eyes, and in the evening twilight, in a sky that is already dim, I make out three black shadows: the three crosses. My Son died on one of them! My Son! It was his death bed! His Mother, who had prepared such a lovely cradle for Him while awaiting his birth, and who had suffered so much in being obliged to place Him, for his first sleep, in a cradle of prickly straw, his Mother had to watch Him die on this very hard wood.

Oh! Mothers who cry while thinking of the agony of your departed children, imagine my sorrow! Ponder on it, all of you, women with tender hearts, even if you are not mothers. Ponder on it, all of you honest men who can feel goodness, and you that are bad, if you are not entirely brutes or completely sold into evil, ponder on my sorrow and have pity!

They drag me to make me enter the gate which is on the point of being closed. Behold Jerusalem..., the step-mother who killed the Son of her Spouse! The cruel murderess who has thrown herself on the defenseless being to slaughter him! The thief who waited for him in the narrow way to capture him and steal from him his single treasure: life.

While a Man, my Jesus had only that treasure. He was poor, without money, without gems, without possessions, without means. Since He had accepted his condition as a servant of humanity to guide blind man towards God, He no longer even had his little maternal home, or the bed that was built for him by his putative father, or the bread baked by his Mother. He would sleep wherever a pitying soul took him in; He would eat where someone of good will gave him a bite, without which it was the grasses of the fields that accepted his tired body; it was the starry firmament that watched over his sleep; it was wild berries and the wheat in the fields, the same that nourish the birds, that took care of his hunger. He didn't possess anything more than a sparrow who searches for nourishment in the fields and for his rest in a barn.

But He was young and healthy. He had life.... And they removed it from him! Jerusalem stole this life from him. Like a vampire, Jerusalem sucked all of his blood; like a vulture she wounded him with the beak of her malice; she tortured and pierced him like a sadistic rebel, rejoicing in each of his spasms, in each of his sobs, his tremors, in each of his convulsions. Oh! I still see them...!

Not many people in the streets. After the crime the evil-doers hide themselves, but those, very rarely, who appear for an instant in the narrow streets disappear immediately behind the little doors that they close in a hurry, as if they fear a hostile interruption. They make me shudder from horror.... That young man perhaps blasphemed him, and that thick-set muscular man perhaps mistreated and beat him.... Now they run away, they hide, they entrench themselves. They are afraid. Of what? Of a dead man. For them, it's only a dead man, because they've denied that He is God. Then, what are they afraid of? On whom are they closing their doors? To remorse. To punishment.

It's all worthless. The remorse is in you and will follow you eternally. The punishment is not human, and against it your locks and your barricades are useless. This punishment comes from heaven, it comes from God, from Him who avenges his immolated Son, who penetrates in through your walls and doors, and with his omnipotent ray will mark you for the supernatural chastisement that awaits you. The world will come to the Christ, to the Son of God who is also mine. The world will come to the One you have pierced, but you, you will be the Cains of God, marked for eternity, the disgrace of the human race.

And I who am also of your race, who am the Mother of all, I must say that for myself, your Daughter, you have been the most unworthy of fathers. Among my innumerable children you are the ones that have made my care for you the most difficult because you are dirty with the abject dirt of the ones who killed my Child, and don't regret what they have done, while saying: "You were the Messiah, we recognize You, and we adore You."

A patrol of Roman soldiers crosses the road. The rulers fear a raging mob. Oh! Don't have a single fear! These people here are only hyenas, cowardly hyenas. They throw themselves on the defenseless Lamb, but they fear the lion armed with lances and authority. Don't be afraid of these furtive carrion eaters. Your cadenced step causes them to run, and the glint from your lances makes them more timid than rabbits.

But those lances...! One of them opened the heart of my Son! Which one? Simply seeing them tears my heart out. Yet, I would like to have them all in my trembling hands to see which one still bears traces of blood, and to say: "Here it is. Give it to me, soldier! Give it to a mother, in memory of your mother who lives far away. I will pray for her and for you." No soldier would have denied it to me, because they, the men of war, have been the most respectful before the agony of the Son and that of the Mother.

There is the house.... How many hours or how many ages have passed since I entered it last night? Since I have come out of it this morning? Is it really me, the 50-year-old Mother, or an ancestor dating back several centuries, a woman from the early times, rich in ages that have accumulated on her stooped shoulders and on her white-haired head? I have the impression of having lived all of the sorrow of the world and of feeling it now on my shoulders, that bend under its weight. Invisible cross, but so heavy to carry! Cross of stone. Cross heavier than that of my Jesus, perhaps, because I carry his and mine, with the memory of his laceration and the reality of my own laceration.

We enter, because we must enter. But it is not a relief. It is an augmenting of sorrow. Through this door, my Son entered for his last meal. Through this door, He went out to meet his death. He had to put his foot there, where the traitor put his when he left to go call the executioners of the Innocent One.

I saw Judas against this door.... I saw Judas...! And I didn't curse him. I talked to him like a mother with a broken heart, torn over the Son who is good, and over the son who is bad.... I saw Judas...! In him I saw the demon! I, who have always held Lucifer under my heel, and while looking only at God, I never lowered my glance to Satan, I knew his face when I looked at the traitor.... I talked to the devil.... He ran away, because the devil cannot stand the sound of my voice.

Oh! Let me enter the room where my Jesus ate his last meal! There, where the voice of my Child pronounced his last words of peace!

Open! Open this door! You can't close it to a mother! To a mother who would like to breathe in the air, the odor of the breath, the odor of the body of her Son. Don't you know that this breath, this body, it's me? I gave it to him. It's me. It's myself. I carried him for nine months. It's me who gave birth to him, nourished him with my milk, helped him to grow, nursed him. That breath is mine! That scent of his person is also mine! It truly is my own that has become more beautiful in him, my Jesus. Let me smell this odor again one more time! I have in my eyes the image of his Blood and in my nose the odor of his martyred corpse. Let me look at the table where He leaned while He was alive and whole; let me smell the perfume of his youthful Body.

Open! Don't bury Him again for a third time! You've hidden Him from me beneath aromas and bandages. You've closed Him away from me on the other side of the stone. Now, why do you want to deny a mother the possibility of finding his last souvenir, the last trace of him in the breath He left on the other side of this door? Why?

Let me enter. I will search on the floor, on the table, on the chair, the mark of his feet, of his hands; I will cover it with kisses, even wearing my lips completely away.... I will search.... I will perhaps end up finding a hair from his blond head. A hair that is not wet with blood. Do you at least know what this represents for a mother, a hair from the son that death has torn from her? You, Mary Cleopas, and you, Salome, you are certainly mothers, and you don't understand?

John! John! Listen to me. I am now your Mother. It's Him who decided that. Him! You owe me obedience. Open! I love you, John. I have always loved you because you loved Him. I will love you even more, but open. Open, I say. You don't want to? You don't want to? Ah! I no longer have any son, then? Jesus never refused me anything because He was my Son. You refuse. You are not one. You don't understand my sorrow...! John, forgive me...! Open.... Don't cry.... Open....

Jesus! Jesus! Listen to me! Let your Spirit accomplish this miracle! Open for your poor Mother this door that no one wants to open! Jesus, Jesus! I'm fainting.... I'm dying.... I am coming with You, Jesus.... Jesus....»

...And Mary, after having battered against the door with her little fists to try to open it, bends, paler than a lily, after steadying herself by leaning on the women and John. She would fall to the floor if she were not held up and brought to the next room.

Thus ends the vision that accompanied me throughout this dictation.

An hour of preparation for death

July 14, 1946.

Jesus teaches us how to approach death.

Jesus says:

"I have dictated a Holy Hour for those who were wanting it. I have taken the veil from my Hour of Agony in Gethsemani to give you a great prize, because there is no greater act of confidence between friends than that of revealing to the friend one's own suffering. The smile and the kiss are not the supreme proof of love, but tears and pain made known to the friend are. You, my friend, have known this. Since you were with Me in Gethsemani. And now you are on the Cross. And you feel the pains of death. Lean on your Lord, while He gives you an Hour of Preparation for Death."

I.

"My Father, if it is possible, let his chalice pass from me."

This is not one of the seven Words from the Cross. But it is already a word of passion. It is the first act of the passion which is beginning. It is the necessary preparation for the other phases of the holocaust. It is the calling upon the Giver of life, it is resignation; it is humility. It is the prayer in which the will of the spirit and the frailty of the creature who loathes death are intertwined, while the flesh becomes ennobled and the soul perfected.

"Father...!" Oh! This is the hour when the world distances itself far from senses and from thought, while, as a descending meteor, the thought of the other life, of the unknown, of judgement, draws near. And man, ever a little child even if a hundred years old, seeks the bosom of God like a frightened babe left all alone.

Husband, wife, brothers, children, parents, friends....

They were everything, as long as life was far from death, as long as death was a thought hidden under distant mists. But now that death comes forth from beneath the veil and advances, lo, through an overturning of the situation, it is the parents, the wife who lose their distinctive traits, their emotional value, and they grow dim before the imminent advance of death. Like voices which grow faint due to their remoteness, everything of the earth loses strength, as that grows in strength which is of the beyond, that which up until yesterday appeared so very far away.... And a surge of fear strikes the creature.

If it were not painful and fearsome, death would not be the ultimate chastisement and the ultimate means of expiation granted to man. Until the Fall, death was not death, but a falling asleep. And where there was no fall, there was no death, as was the case for Mary Most Holy. I died because all Sin was upon Me, and I have experienced what it is to loathe death.

"Father!" Oh! This God, so many times not loved, or last to be loved, after the heart has loved relatives and friends, or has had more unworthy loves for creatures of vice, or has loved things as gods; this God so often forgotten, and who has tolerated our forgetting Him, who has left us free to forget Him, who has let us have our way, who has at times been scoffed at, at other times cursed, at others denied; it is He who rises up again in the thought of man and takes back his rights. He thunders: "I am!" and in order not to cause one to die of fear through the revelation of his power, He softens this powerful "I am" with a sweet word: "Father."

"I am your Father." There is no longer any terror. The sentiment which this word produces is abandonment.

I, I who had to die, who understood what it is to die, after having taught men to live calling the Most High Yahweh "Father", see then that I have taught you to die without terror, calling "Father" the God who rises again or makes Himself more present to the spirit of him who is dying amidst the spasms of agony.

"Father!" Do not fear. You who are dying, do not fear this God who is Father! He does not approach as a judge, armed with judgement book and axe. He does not approach as a cynic, snatching you away from life and loves. He comes opening his arms to you, saying: "Come back to your home. Come to rest. I will pay you back with interest for what you are leaving here behind. And I promise you this: on behalf of those you are leaving behind, in my bosom you will be more active than if you remain here below in a struggle which is frenzied, and not always rewarded with success."

But death is always sorrow. Sorrow by virtue of the physical suffering, sorrow by virtue of the moral suffering, sorrow by virtue of the spiritual suffering. Here is something I already said: death must be sorrow for there to be a means of ultimate expiation in time. And in a swirl of mists, which through alternating events, blot out and reveal what in life has been cherished and what in life made us fearful of the realities beyond, the soul, the mind, and the heart, like a ship seized in a great tempest, pass from calm areas—already in the peace of the imminent port now close at hand, within sight, and so serene that it already gives a blessed tranquility and a sense of repose like that of one who, having come almost to the end of a wearisome labor, anticipates the joy of the rest which is at hand—they pass into a zone where the tempest buffets them, strikes them and causes them to suffer, to fear, to groan. It is again the world, the frenzied world with all its tentacles: the family, the business. It is the anguish of the death struggle. It is the fear of the final step.... And then? And then...? Darkness overruns and suffocates the light; it hisses its terrors.... Where any longer is heaven? Why death? Why must one die? And a death rattle is already in the throat: "I don't want to die!"

No, my dying brothers, you die because to die is just, to die is holy, being the will of God. No. Do not cry out so! This shout does not come from your soul. It is the Enemy who influences your weakness to make you say this. Change the rebellious and cowardly shout into a cry of love and trust: "Father, if it is possible, let this chalice pass from me." Like the rainbow after the storm, look how this cry brings back the light, the calm. See heaven once again, the holy reasons for dying, the reward of dying, that is, the return to the Father. Understand that the spirit, too, the spirit indeed has greater rights than the flesh because it is immortal and supernatural in nature, and therefore has precedence over the flesh. Then speak the word which is absolution for all your sins of rebellion: "Nevertheless, not my will but yours be done."

This, then, is peace; this, then, is victory. The angel of God draws close to you, and comforts you because you have won the battle that makes you ready to turn your death into a triumph.

II.

"Father, forgive them."

This is the moment for stripping yourself of all that is heavy in order to fly more surely to God. You cannot take with you either feelings or riches which are not spiritual and good. And there will never be a man who dies without having something to forgive one or more of his fellow men, in many things, for many reasons.

What man arrives at death without having suffered the harshness of a betrayal, the harshness of a dislike, the harshness of a lie, of an extortion, of some sort of injury on the part of relatives, associates, or friends? Well then: this is the time to forgive in order to be forgiven. To forgive completely, letting go not only of the rancor, not only the memory, but also the conviction that our reason for indignation was just. This is the hour of death. Time, world, business, feelings, are at an end. Everything becomes "nothing." One sole truth now exists: God. What is the use, then, of bringing beyond the doorstep that which belongs on this side?

Forgive. And since to arrive at the perfection of love and of pardon—which does not any longer say: "And yet I had good reason"—is very, is too-difficult for man, so then, pass on to the Father the task of pardoning for us. Let us hand over our pardon to Him, to Him who is not man, who is perfect, who is good, who is Father, so that He may place it in his Fire, and give it perfected to whoever merits the pardon.

Forgive the living and the dead. Yes. Even the dead, who have been occasions of pain. Their death has taken away many painful twinges from the anger caused by the offenses; sometimes it has taken them all away. But the memory still lasts. They made us suffer; and we remember that they made us suffer. This memory always puts a limit on our forgiveness. No. Not any longer, now. Now death is about to take away all limitations to the spirit. We are entering into the infinite. Remove, therefore, even this memory which puts a limit on forgiveness. Forgive, forgive so that the soul may have no weight and torment of memories, and can be at peace with all its brothers, living or suffering, before meeting with the Peaceful One.

"Father, forgive them." Holy humility, sweet love of pardon granted, which implies pardon asked of God for trespasses against God and against neighbor, trespasses on the part of him who is asking pardon for his brothers. Act of love. To die in an act of love is to have the forbearance of love. Blessed are those who know how to pardon in expiation for all their hardness of heart and sins of anger.

III.

"Behold your son."

Behold your son! Surrender that which is dear, with

farsighted and holy intention. Give up affections, and surrender yourself to God without resistance. Do not be envious of those who possess what we are leaving behind. With a word you can entrust to God all that you cherish and which you are leaving behind, and everything that worries you, even your own spirit.

Remember the Father who is Father. Place into his hands the spirit which is returning to the Source. Say: "Behold! Here I am. Take me with You because I give myself. I am not surrendering by force of circumstances. I am giving myself because I love You as a son returning to his father."

And say: "Here then. These are my dear ones. I give them to You. These are my deeds, which sometimes have caused me to be unjust, envious of my neighbor, and which have caused me to forget You, because they seemed to me so important—they actually were, but I believed them to be even more so—they seemed to me to be of capital importance for the well-being of my loved ones, for my honor, for the esteem which they brought to me. I believed also that I alone was able to look after them. I believed that I was necessary for their accomplishment. Now I see.... I was nothing more than a microscopic device in the perfect universe of your Providence, and quite often a faulty device, which impaired the work of the perfect universe. Now that the lights and the voices of the world are ceasing, and all is moving off into the distance, I see.... I hear.... How inadequate my works were, how tattered, how incomplete! How far they were from the Good. I have presumed to be somebody. It was you—foreseeing, provident, holy—who corrected my labors and made them useful once again. I have been overconfident. Sometimes I have even said that You did not love me because I did not succeed in what I wanted to do as did some others whom I envied. Now I see. Have mercy on me!"

Humble abandonment, grateful reflection on Providence in reparation for your acts of presumption, greed, envy, and for replacing God with poor human possessions, and with gluttony for sundry riches.

IV.

"Remember me!"

You have accepted the chalice of death, you have pardoned, you have yielded what was yours, even yourselves. You have greatly mortified the "I" of man, greatly liberated the soul from that which displeases God: from the spirit of rebellion, from the spirit of rancor, from the spirit of greed. You have yielded life, justice, ownership—poor life, poorer justice, thrice-poor human ownership—to the Lord. Like the languishing prophet, Job, you lie destitute before God. And so you are able to say: "Remember me."

You are no longer anything. Not health, not dignity, not richness. You no longer possess even your own selves. You are like a caterpillar which can become a butterfly or else rot in the prison of your body, to the ultimate and extreme injury of the spirit. You are dust which returns to dust, or dust which is changing into a star. According to your choice you can ascend into the vortex of God. The final hour decides eternal life. Keep that in mind. And cry out, "Remember me!"

God awaits this cry from poor Job to fill him to the brim with blessings of his Kingdom. It is sweet to a Father to forgive, to intervene, to console. He waits only for this cry to say to you: "I am with you, son. Do not be afraid." Say it, to make amends for all the times you may have been forgetful of the Father, or you may have been too proud.

V.

"My God, why have you abandoned me?"

Sometimes it seems that the Father abandons. This is only so that He may increase expiation and give greater pardon while hidden. Can man angrily complain of this, man who has an infinite number of times abandoned God? And must he despair because God tests him?

How many things have you kept in your heart which were not God! How many times have you been sluggish with Him! In how many matters have you rejected Him and driven Him away! You have filled your heart with everything. And then you have nailed it closed, and well padlocked. You were afraid that God, by entering in, might be able to disturb your lazy quietism, might be able to purify his temple by driving away the usurpers. As long as you were happy, what did it matter to you to have God? You were saying: "I have everything because, of course, I deserve it." And then when you were not happy, did you never flee from God, and make Him the cause of all your misfortunes?

Oh! Unfair children who drink poison, who walk into labyrinths, who plunge headlong into ravines and into lairs of serpents and other wild beasts, and then say: "It is God who is to blame." If God were not Father and a holy Father, what should He respond to the lament you utter in your painful hours, if in the hours of contentment you forgot Him? Oh! Unfair children who, full of faults, would pretend to be treated as the Son of God himself was not treated in the hour of the holocaust, pray tell, who was the more abandoned? In order to save you, was not the Christ, the Innocent One, He who accepted absolute abandonment by God after having always loved Him so devotedly? And is it not you who bear the name of "Christians"? And do you not have the duty of saving at least yourselves? There is not salvation in turbid sloth pleased with itself and dreading the annoyance of accepting the Active One.

Imitate Christ, then, by uttering this cry in the moment of greatest anguish. But make sure that the note of the cry be a note of meekness and humility, not a note of blasphemy and rebuke. "Why have You abandoned me, You who know that without You I can do nothing? Come, O Father, come to save me. Come to give me strength to save myself, because the pangs of death are horrible and the Adversary cunningly increases his power over me. He hisses to me that You no longer love me. Make yourself felt, O Father, not through my merits but precisely because I am a nothing, without merit, who does not know how to conquer if he is alone, and who understands now that life was work for heaven."

Woe to him who is alone, it is said. Woe to him who is alone at the hour of death, alone with himself against Satan and the flesh! But do not fear. If you cry out to the Father, He will come. And this humble calling upon Him will expiate your culpable sluggishness toward God, the false piety, the unruly self-love, which caused you to be slothful.

VI.

"I thirst."

Yes, indeed, when the true value of eternal life is understood as opposed to the false worth of earthly life, when the purification through pain and through death is accepted in holy obedience, when one has grown in wisdom and grace before God in a few hours, sometimes in a few minutes, more than one would have grown in many years of life, there comes a deep thirst for heavenly waters, for heavenly things. The lusts of all human thirsts are overcome. There comes the supernatural thirst to possess God. The thirst for love. The soul aspires to drink love and to be imbibed by love. As a rain which has fallen upon the soil and does not want to become dust but to return as mist, the soul now has a thirst to ascend to the place from which it came down. The walls of the flesh nearly broken, the prisoner feels the gentle breezes from the place of its origin, and longs for it with all its being.

What sort of an exhausted pilgrim, who finally sees close at hand his native place after years, would not gather his forces and journey on, nimbly, tenaciously, heedless of everything but arriving from the place he one day took his leave, where he left behind all his true good? Now he is certain of finding it and of relishing it much more, because in his exile he has experienced the paltry good which does not satiate.

"I thirst." Thirst for You, my God. Thirst to be with You. Thirst to possess You. Thirst to give You. Because on the threshold between earth and heaven one really knows how to understand love for one's neighbor as it should be understood. And there comes the desire to act in order to give God to the neighbor we are leaving behind. This is the holy activity of the saints, dead seeds which become ears of grain. They pour themselves out in love, in order to give love, and to make God loved by those who are still in the struggles of earth! "I thirst." When the soul arrives on the doorstep of Life, there is only one water which slakes the thirst for good: the Living Water, God Himself. True Love: God Himself. Love opposed to egoism.

For those who are just, egoism is dead before the flesh, and love reigns. And love cries out: "I thirst for You and for souls. To save. To love. To die, in order to be free to love and to save. To die, in order to be born. To relinquish in order to possess. To renounce all sweetness, every comfort, because here below everything is vanity, and the soul wants only to plunge into the river, into the ocean of the Divinity, and drink of It, be in It, without further thirst, because the Fount of the Water of Life will have received it. Have this thirst in order to make reparation for the lack of love, and for lust.

VII.

"All is accomplished."

All the renunciations, all the sufferings, all the trials, the struggles, the victories, the offerings: everything. There is nothing left but to present oneself to God. The time granted to the creature to become a god, for Satan to tempt him, is complete. The pain ceases, the testing ceases, the struggle ceases. There remain only the judgement and the loving purification; or there comes, most blessedly, the undelayed abode of heaven. But whatever is earth, whatever is human will, comes to an end. All is accomplished! The word of complete resignation or of joyous recognition at having finished the trial and consummated the holocaust.

I am not considering those who die in mortal sin. As regards such, they do not say "All is accomplished", but it is said on their behalf by the victorious angel of darkness with a shriek of victory, and by the defeated angel, with a wail of sorrow.

I am speaking to penitent sinners, to good Christians, or to those who became heroes of virtue. These human beings, more and more alive in the spirit as bit by bit death takes over the flesh, murmur or shout, in resignation or in joy: "All is accomplished. The sacrifice has ended. Take it as my expiation! Take it as my offering of love!" Thus the spirits speak their penultimate word, according to whether they undergo death by virtue of the universal law, or offer it as a voluntary sacrifice from a victim soul. But no less in the first case than in the second, they now arrive at liberation from matter; they recline the spirit on the bosom of God, saying: "Father, into your hands I commend my spirit."

"Maria, do you know what it is to expire with this sublimity in the heart? It is to expire in the kiss of God. There are many preparations for death. But believe that this one, based on my words, in its simplicity is the holiest."

Maria Valtorta's works are published by

Centro Editoriale Valtortiano
03036 Isola del Liri - Italia
Telefono 776.807032
Fax 776.809789

Distributor for Canada and USA:

MÉDIASPAUL

250, Saint-François Nord, Sherbrooke, QC, J1E 2B9 (Canada)
Tél: (819) 569-5535 – Fax: (819) 565-5474